Anna Mathur is a mother of three and an experienced psychotherapist accredited by the British Association for Counselling and Psychotherapy. She is passionate about taking therapy out of the therapy room and empowering people to utilise simple techniques that will help them reframe the way that they think. She is the author of *Mind Over Mother*.

Anna Mathur

KNOW

Your

WORTH

How to build your self-esteem,
grow in confidence and worry less
about what people think

PIATKUS

PIATKUS

First published in Great Britain in 2021 by Piatkus

1 3 5 7 9 10 8 6 4 2

A CIP catalogue record for this book
is available from the British Library.

ISBN 978-0-349-42814-7

Typeset in Bembo by M Rules
Printed and bound in Great Britain by Clays Ltd, Elcograf S.p.A

Papers used by Piatkus are from well-managed forests
and other responsible sources.

Piatkus
An imprint of
Little, Brown Book Group
Carmelite House
50 Victoria Embankment
London EC4Y 0DZ

An Hachette UK Company
www.hachette.co.uk

www.littlebrown.co.uk

Note: The names of the people who share their experiences
in this book have been changed to protect their privacy.

For my children, Oscar, Charlie and Florence.
I will for ever work on my self-esteem so that I may
always believe I am worthy of you.

Contents

Introduction

Let me start with two observations that are not open to negotiation. Sure, I may not know you in person, but here are a couple of things that I know about you with absolute certainty:

- You are worthy of good things.
- You deserve rest, laughter, support, good relationships and opportunities.

How might your life be different if you were actually to believe this too, within your core? If it were only straightforward to believe the truth sometimes! My hope is that this book will help you to find these non-negotiable truths more believable.

I will be totally honest with you from the outset. This isn't another self-development book in which I'm going to tell you how to be a better person. I don't know about you, but my shelf is already groaning with those. Nor am I going to tell you how to change yourself in order to be better, live better or do better. Instead, we're going to do quite the opposite: this is a self-*undevelopment* book.

Let me explain. As a therapist, a lot of people come to speak with me because they want to be 'more'. They want to be happier, more confident around others and more comfortable being themselves. Many of them are seeking to have more control over anxiety, or find an end to self-sabotaging and feelings of imposter syndrome. They come to me hungering for more meaningful relationships and clarity.

When we peel away the onion layers of our thoughts, experiences and different ways of coping, and when we take the time to examine the hurdles that make it hard for us to develop good habits, we discover that the biggest hurdle of them all is this: we don't believe we are worthy of good things. Instead, we believe that our worth is the result of what we do, how well we do it and what others think of us. This has been the story of generations before us and it is constantly being reinforced throughout our lives.

The truth is, you are not the sum of what you do. As a baby, you didn't question your worth. You had no shame in crying out for milk, warmth or comfort. You didn't worry about being a burden on the arms that carried you, nor did you battle waves of guilt when someone steamed carrots for your lunch. You were comfortable with your worth and you didn't question it. But as you grew up, you became aware that the world and its people treated you in different ways, wanting different things for you and from you. Your understanding of your worth – and with it, your self-esteem – began to change.

Your self-esteem is the foundation upon which all of your decisions are made, your relationships are formed and you tackle every one of life's curveballs. It determines where you set the level of your expectations and limits, and whether you respect these. It dictates whether you find it easy to talk about your feelings and needs, and how you let others treat you. It's the deciding factor in how you relate to yourself and how you deal with both criticism and love.

My words in this book are not going to tell you how to be enough. No, I am going to guide you through the process of stripping away everything that taught you that you are not enough as you are. Sometimes the best and most life-affirming growth occurs through a chipping away, a stripping back to reveal the core that lay hidden there all along. Your real worth never changed, but your awareness of it did.

Why I've written this book for you

Shiny ads and social-media streams emit the siren call of: 'If you buy this or do that, you will become a happier, more likeable version of yourself.' We are constantly being given the message that we need to change ourselves in order to become more acceptable to the world. Yet like a fast-food meal, nothing satisfies us for long. Compliments lose their clout, shiny new possessions become outdated, and the buzz of a promotion dissipates. Friendship groups ebb and flow. Nothing gives us the long-term sense of validation we are seeking.

The problem is that we've been trying to self-improve our way to a sense of self-worth. But if we want to be more confident, we need to explore our authentic and inherent self-worth. If we want to be able to say 'no', we need to understand how our worth allows us to assert our boundaries. If failure shakes us, we need to appreciate that our worth means it's okay to get things wrong. If we fear being a burden, we need to explore why we are worthy of kindness. If we find it hard to ask for help, we need to explore how our worth allows us to be supported. If we find ourselves in toxic relationships, we need to appreciate why we are worthy of healthy ones. If we find ourselves tired and resentful, we need to accept that we are worthy of rest. If we feel like an imposter, we should understand how we are worthy of our success. If we find it hard to share our opinions, we need to consider our worthiness to have these heard. And I could go on . . . !

My hope is that after reading this book, you will come to know your self-worth and find it easier to implement helpful coping mechanisms and habits. I also hope that you'll experience how the relentless desire to 'be better' and 'do more' diminishes as you realise that perhaps you are actually already far more acceptable than you first thought.

My story

Do you know what has made me feel uncomfortable for much of my life? Love. Love and other good things. Isn't that a shame? The things that should have made my life enjoyable and most worth living have been the hardest for me to receive. I was always loved; there is no doubt about that. And I'm very privileged to have always had people in my life who have treated me with kindness and respect. However, there have been certain key figures who have loved me but who, due to their own childhood and life experiences, couldn't love me well. This called my sense of worth into question and set me upon a path in which I felt I had to earn love.

I've fought relentlessly to feel worthy of good things. I have tried to be better, stronger, wiser, more confident, clever, resilient and attractive. I've given the last scraps of myself and let my boundaries be steamrollered in order to please people. I've deprioritised my needs so many times that I've often lost sight of what they were. I've felt like an imposter in my own life, wearing so many masks in order to be accepted that I began to question who was behind them. I believed the real me wasn't good enough, clever enough, like-able enough. I always had to add value. I always had to try harder.

The truth is that your worth doesn't change. But your understanding of it sure can.

And then I realised that I never felt enough – because I wasn't. It was incredibly liberating to realise that I am not enough. Nor are you. None of us will ever be enough. We will never be enough to be acceptable to the whole world. You will never have enough energy to fulfil every role you take on, to the standard you want. You will never be enough to please the whole world, because you are an individual with limited resources. But you can certainly go to your grave exhausted through trying; I just don't want you to! The truth is that your worth doesn't change. But your understanding of it sure can. And that is what we're going to do here, in this book. We're going to unlearn what we've been taught about our worth.

Working on my self-esteem has been and continues to be the most worthwhile investment of my time. Because regardless of my fluctuating feelings, I now dare to believe that I am worthy of the good things in my life – from the hugs of my children and the opportunity to write this book, to the dinner I prepared for my family. The belief that I am worthy of them allows me to enjoy them.

So, whether your self-esteem is wavering, it dips and dives like a rollercoaster, or is sitting at rock bottom, there is hope. While I cannot change what you have been through, the way you have been treated or what you have been taught about yourself in the past, I can help you see yourself differently. It is absolutely possible to transform the way you understand your worth. And I tell you, there will not be a corner of your life that will remain untouched and unchanged when you do.

Being the therapist and the client

I gained a master's degree in psychotherapy and counselling at Regent's University London. There I began my journey to becoming an accredited psychotherapist. I've worked in many contexts – from GP surgeries, to the squishy blue sofa in my living room at my home in Surrey. My clients and I do deep and dynamic work together, as well as 'tell me about your relationships with your parents' work.

I now see private clients at home and in clinics. I've loved getting back into the swing of it between three maternity leaves. After having my second baby, I experienced awful sleep-deprivation and a dark time of post-natal depression. I felt more of a failure than ever. I'd spent my career supporting others, yet I somehow couldn't muster the energy to believe there would be light at the end of the tunnel. (Spoiler alert — we *all* need support from others, and knowledge doesn't protect you from facing challenges of your own!)

In 2019, whilst my newborn baby slept, I wrote *Mind Over Mother: Every Mum's Guide to Worry and Anxiety in the First Years*. I wanted to prevent other mums from having their experience of motherhood warped by anxiety. With the increased openness on social media about mum-guilt and worry, there's been a collective sigh of relief that nobody is suffering alone. However, as a therapist, I also wanted fellow mothers to know that they can regain the headspace that worry and guilt all too often consume. With the book finally on the shelves, I started working on my other passion: to inspire people to address issues around self-esteem.

Over the last few years, I have spoken to hundreds of women on a one-to-one basis. I've spoken to mums as they've sought solace while sitting in the car on the drive-way, and to CEOs whispering on their phones from the boardroom. Most of my clients know full well what steps might help them, such as implementing new habits and boundaries, or seeking clarity in certain aspects of their life. However, they've all hit an invisible hurdle, which stops them from doing the things they know will benefit them. This hurdle may take different forms — such as a lack of confidence, imposter syndrome, chronic busyness, exhaustion, overwhelm, fear or anxiety – but fundamentally they all have their roots firmly in the same place: low self-esteem.

We can have all the tools and resources, books, podcasts and techniques we like at our fingertips, but unless we dare to believe we are worthy of the kindness, patience, gentleness and support required both from others and – here's the challenge – from ourselves, to allow change to occur, we'll struggle to make it far down that road. Many of my clients try so hard to change things and end up criticising themselves when they don't progress as quickly as they'd like, or find it as easy to implement new habits as they'd hoped. But I discovered that when all of the 'trying' was put aside for a while, so that they could focus instead on the relationship they *actually* did have with themselves (rather than on the one they wanted), everything else began to shift naturally too.

For many years I'd been working on the symptoms rather than the cause – both in myself and with clients. Now, I believe I've found the missing link. A root cause of low self-esteem was the reason why so many of my clients' efforts to change seemed to work for a while, before another kind of anxiety would pop up in the place of their original problem, or a new wave of overwhelm would roll in. We can relentlessly throw water at the flames of a fire, but only when we address the source of the fire itself will the flames be extinguished. In this book, I want to help you tackle the source of your fires. To lessen the waves of overwhelm rather than to fear them. And to soften that sense of imposter syndrome rather than just offer you tips that help to shut it down momentarily.

There is a little, yet potentially life-changing, tick-box requirement when training to be a therapist. It's the need to appoint a therapist of your own. I have had therapy myself, on and off, for over ten years now, because I often end up hitting challenges that reveal another layer that I need to work on. It's hard work, but it's worthwhile. And the topic I always end up touching on, within my therapy sessions, is that of self-worth and self-esteem. The fact is that every friend, client and family member benefits from my healthier self-esteem. So, I am a therapist in therapy, and I will continue to do this sort of inner work so that I can make good decisions, hold my boundaries, revel in the love from my family, enjoy the good times and recognise I'm worthy of support in the tough ones. I know this road from experience and I am not here to point you towards some distant panacea, but to invite you on the journey with me.

How to get the most out of this book

We are about to begin the journey towards building your confidence and finding some much-deserved freedom from your fear of what others think about you. In chapter 1, I'm going to begin by guiding you through a self-esteem MOT, which will be an opportunity for you to check where your self-esteem is currently at. Then, in the chapter that follows, we will journey through the whys and the whats of low self-esteem to help you understand why you feel the way you do, what perpetuates your issues around self-worth and what low self-esteem has cost you.

Knowing the 'whys' will give us a good foundation from which to move into the 'well, what now?' stage. Understanding more about how you tick will shine a gentle light on those areas of your life that would benefit from a little more care and encouragement. I'm going to be sharing lots of insights that you can implement over time to take your self-esteem on a healthy and fulfilling upwards spiral. When we address issues of self-worth, we are looking at the habits of a lifetime — so take the journey at your own pace. If you feel you'd benefit from further support, turn to Helpful Contacts, page 265, to find some recommendations.

In this book, you will also find the following sections:

Journal points

At the end of each chapter, you will find questions to con-template and answer in a journal. They are designed to help you reflect on the insights in this book, and to make these relevant to your own life. Writing things down helps the brain process them in a different way, but if you don't enjoy writing, you can simply think about your answers. Respond to the questions in whichever way you like.

Mantras

I love a good mantra! These are small takeaway sentences that you can memorise and recall whenever you need encouragement or grounding.

Quotes

The voices of my social-media community are peppered throughout this book, as I asked for their comments on various topics. All names have been changed and everyone shared their responses knowing they might be included in the following chapters.

Chapter 1

Your self-esteem MOT

Mantra: *Good self-esteem isn't 'me first', it's 'me too'.*

And so we begin. I don't know about you, but I feel far more motivated to address something once I've begun to realise the impact it has on my life. When you begin to see the true cost that low self-esteem has had on how you feel about yourself, how you relate to others and how you make decisions, I'm hoping that working on it will climb to the top of your list of priorities.

This chapter is your self-esteem MOT. Many of the things that we want to improve, such as low confidence, or feeling exhausted by the constant drive to please others, are different-coloured flowers with the same root. When you address self-esteem, those things change too.

What are self-worth and self-esteem?

Self-worth is your worth as a person. It doesn't change. Let's imagine you are worth, say, 1 point. Regardless of who you are, what you possess, how loved you are or what you achieve with your life, you're still worth that 1 point. A coin has the same value whether it's fresh from the Royal Mint, or greasy and chipped at the edges.

Self-esteem, however, is how you understand your worth. It's not fixed but changes and evolves, fluctuating day by day. It may skyrocket with a compliment or plummet with a failing. Your self-esteem is like the car windscreen; it's the window through which you view both your self-worth and the world around you. As you drive along, it gets covered in rain, dust, mud splatters and dead bugs. Working on self-esteem is like turning on the windscreen wipers to keep cleaning the screen, so that you can view your worth more clearly. When you switch them off, the windscreen becomes spattered and misty, distorting how you see yourself and the world around you.

False confidence

We will be looking at confidence in much more detail in chapter 10, but I just want to touch on the subject of false confidence here. Often we idealise confidence as a personality trait, but I find it helpful to recognise how low self-esteem can be hidden by false confidence. All isn't always as it seems. False confidence isn't the type of self-belief that bubbles up from a feeling of being comfortable with who you are, but a need to fake confidence or status in order to feel more acceptable to others.

False confidence may come across as an obsession with

status, boastfulness, defensiveness, loudness or a lack of
humility, but it actually has low self-esteem at its core.
Similarly, self-underestimation is when someone believes
they are of low worth. Both false confidence and self-
underestimation can have their origins in how we were
brought up.

The ideal

In an ideal world, our caregivers would have treated themselves and others with respect while we were growing up.
They would have respected their own and other people's
boundaries and limitations, and shown an awareness of the
feelings and needs of others. When this sort of behaviour is
modelled for us from a young age, we are much more likely
to develop a similar level of respect for ourselves and others.

In such an ideal world, you'd come to respect and value
yourself as much as you do others. You'd have boundaries
that encourage others to treat you with respect too. You'd
respect your needs, feelings, limitations and your voice.
You'd be comfortable with the fact that sometimes you need
support. You'd be yourself without apology, yet apologise
freely should your actions hurt others. Feedback would
be considered, and acted upon as appropriate. You'd feel
healthy pride at your successes, and learn humbly from your
failures. You'd give within your limited means, and then
rest in order to refuel.

There's so much buzz about self-love. It would be wonderful if you loved yourself, but for too many of us love

feels like a tall order. At times, in my own experience, an invitation to love myself would have felt impossible. I'm not going to be asking you to love yourself, but I'm hoping that you'll develop a new respect for yourself. Think of this book as the nudging of a snowball down a hill. You'll gain momentum as you continue on your way.

Loving yourself need not be the end goal or prize. As with any long-term relationship, our relationship with ourselves is a dance, a wiggly line, a fluctuation in feelings. If I were to expect my marriage to feel like a life-long honeymoon, I'd be sorely disappointed. Feelings come and go, rise and fall; they trundle along amidst the mundane. It's having a firm foundation that really matters. So if you can aim for self-respect as your foundation, you can expect all your other feelings of irritation, annoyance, liking and loving to dance upon that ground.

The winding road

As I've worked on my own self-esteem, my life has changed. Sure, life's curveballs still come at me. However, my relationships have felt more equal and enjoyable, as I've become increasingly confident in respecting my own needs and feelings. But then something will happen – I'll face a challenge, a loss of some sort, or receive a tricky piece of feedback. And it feels like a lightning bolt has struck my core, shattering my self-esteem. I find myself back in a place of

I'm hoping that you'll develop a new respect for yourself.

self-criticism and doubt. *Who am I to think I'm a good person anyway? Who am I to think myself worthy of any opportunity?*

When my first book was published in the spring of 2020, we were in the middle of a global pandemic. All book launch events were cancelled, so I celebrated at home with my husband and kids in lockdown. That day, I found myself amidst a tidal wave of congratulations, with messages from friends and handmade cards from my children. I'd hoped to feel proud and happy, but I was sad to find myself suffering from an overwhelming dose of unworthiness and imposter syndrome. I had spent years working on my self-esteem, and I had hoped I would feel worthy of enjoying the celebration, yet found myself wanting to flee it.

I took a walk through the local woods that afternoon and had a realisation. This was not a set-back, because working on self-esteem isn't a linear process. A few years ago, goodness knows how I'd have dealt with the attention and celebration, or how long it might have taken for me to find some compassion for myself. Progress is sometimes only clear when we take a moment to recognise how far we've come. That's why journaling can be so helpful, allowing us to look back as well as forwards. As a comparison, although I don't witness my daughter growing day by day, when I look at photos from a mere month ago, I see growth. So, as you embark on this process of working on your self-esteem, be gentle with your expectations, and know that growth will sometimes feel like a step back. Now that your expectations are set on wiggly line – rather than a poker-straight one – to chart your progress, let's begin.

The cost of low self-esteem

Imagine stepping into a huge, old mansion. It hasn't been inhabited for centuries. You've been tasked with giving it a thorough going-over so that it can be opened to visitors and enjoyed. You creak open the front door with an old iron key the size of your hand. Your lungs inhale the thick, stale air as your eyes take in the scene. Everything sits in its intended position, yet it's utterly covered in the thick dust of time. The hallways are adorned with alabaster statues, their features distorted by layers of residue. The expanses of wall display valuable oil paintings whose details are blurred by grime. Thick curtains tumble from ceiling to floor, their colours dulled by a coat of grey.

You start to go through each room, opening doors on unoiled hinges and flicking on old metal light switches. Bulbs flicker awake, bathing rooms in orange light. You haul back the curtains, welcoming summer daylight through the wind-battered windows. You begin to clean each surface. You reveal that which was there all along. You reveal the house's true worth.

You see, we are like this home. Culture yells, 'Don't waste time. Knock it down, start over; do it better, newer, shinier.' But we don't need to rip up tiles or replace antique furniture with flat-pack stuff in this house, or in ourselves. What lies underneath the dust is good. It always was. The dust represents the layers of mistreatment, neglect, unrealistic expectations, unkind words, misspent resources and disrespected boundaries that we have encountered. So, let's take a closer look at what was there all along.

In the big old house, you had to clunk on the lights to see what you were working with. That's what we're going to do now. We're going to shine a light on some of the elements of your life that are impacted when your self-esteem is low. Over the next few pages, you'll find descriptions of a number of the characteristics of low self-esteem. Don't surprised if many of them resonate. They have all been relevant for me at one time or another. As you gain clarity on how low self-esteem has impacted you, this will enable you to tackle the situation!

You feel like you need to please others

I always offered to get friends from the airport. I would do whatever I could to be a good friend, even if it meant filling the car up when I didn't have much cash – as I'd never ask for money. After a few years, it hurt that they never offered back.

Cally

As the term suggests, people-pleasing is characterised by the consistent prioritising of pleasing others. Pleasing others can undoubtedly offer a sense of validation and make us feel liked and accepted. But when the aim is to gain validation through pleasing others, you are more likely to end up feeling burnt out and resentful. Perhaps you expend more mental, emotional or physical energy on pleasing others than you actually have to spare, because you place more value on the needs of others than your own.

I call myself a people-pleaser in recovery, because when

my self-esteem takes a dip, I catch myself looking for the sense of validation that comes from pleasing other people. However, people-pleasing brings with it the weighty fear of displeasing others. I have spent many a restless night replaying dinner-party conversations or re-reading text messages, worried that I'd unintentionally annoyed someone. If I suspected I'd displeased someone, the guilt would sit heavily in my stomach for days and have me scrabbling for any way to make things right.

It's not wrong to want to please others. The important thing is that you're aware of the motivation behind the action. When you make sacrifices out of choice rather than a need for validation, you are more likely to be respecting your own boundaries and acknowledging what resources you really have to offer. When you give out of choice, rather than out of a need to feel accepted or validated, you are less likely to end up feeling hurt, resentful or burnt out, and more likely to invest in the kind of relationships that are mutually rewarding.

You feel low in confidence

I feel jealous of people who can be themselves. I always question myself. I wish I could just be myself.

Letty

Low confidence goes hand in hand with low self-esteem. If you believe that your worth is directly correlated to how useful or acceptable you are to those around you, your confidence levels will rise and fall depending on the way people treat you. If your self-esteem rests upon what others think about you (or what you *think* they think about you), this can give you social anxiety. Social anxiety will cause you to put more pressure on yourself to 'get it right' and to please others. You may spend time picking apart social interactions, searching for reassurance you were liked, or fearing you've said something wrong or unintentionally upset someone.

I have often felt lacking in confidence. However, I bet few people have noticed this, as I have become good at *appearing* confident. False confidence has acted as a cover-up for my low self-esteem, because I haven't wanted people to see my vulnerability or worry about me. I have wanted to ensure everyone around me felt at ease, so I'd try to be who I thought they wanted me to be. As a result, I have felt very anxious in social situations, especially when my confidence and self-esteem have been low.

You procrastinate often

I'm so scared of getting a work assignment wrong that I find it hard to even start.

Kay

When your self-esteem is dictated by the quality or quantity of what you do, missing your own high bar comes with a very high cost. You may find yourself avoiding taking on new projects or pieces of work, due to your fear of failure.

Failure doesn't just feel like an event to be overcome, but a statement about who you are.

At university, I'd often delay writing essays because I'd fear failing before I'd even got started. I'd leave it until the last minute, putting myself under immense pressure. I remember racing across campus with freshly printed pages, submitting coursework with seconds to spare. My body was so stressed that I was sick and broke down into tears once I'd crammed the papers into the tutor's pigeonhole. I would blame myself for procrastinating, yet again. I didn't realise at the time that my procrastination was rooted in a fear of getting it wrong.

Being able to write this book shows how far I have come. I give myself pep talks before opening my laptop, telling myself that the important thing is that I get the words down; they don't need to be perfect, they just need to be present. By becoming more accepting of my own imperfection, I no longer fear failure quite so much. It makes it easier to start things.

You are a perfectionist

I can't stand getting stuff wrong at work. One foot out of line and I feel like I've failed and will be found out. My reaction is to work harder and put more pressure on myself.

Edie

Perfectionism is the pursuit of a standard that gets repeatedly nudged out of reach. It's like the dangled carrot in front of the hungry donkey, promising him that his rumbling stomach will be relieved if only he moves that little further forwards. And so he does it again, and again.

Sadly, any boost to self-esteem feels short-lived, like the sugar low that comes after eating a bag of sweets. We hunt for the next hit. Perfectionist standards can be applied to anything, from hobbies to parenting, body shape to the wording of emails. Simple tasks can quickly become opportunities for failure. Failure, self-criticism and shame fill the gap between what you feel you should be achieving, and what you actually do achieve.

It's difficult to reach your own high standards for long enough to boost your self-esteem consistently. Therefore, you're likely to experience more of those feelings of failure than of the positive feelings that come with achievement. The good news is that when you tweak your expectations to acknowledge your limits, the gap that's filled with feelings of failure and self-criticism gets smaller too.

You often compare yourself to others

If I feel crap, social media makes me feel worse. All I see is everyone else doing a great job.

Zara

I don't like to be wrong about myself. I like to think that I know myself best. So if I believe I'm failing at motherhood, I can easily view the world through that lens. I'll scroll through social media and perhaps see a mother frolicking through lavender fields, surrounded by her smiling, clean kids. In that moment, my feelings are confirmed: I'm doing a worse job than her.

It's hard to see others in a realistic light when we view ourselves through the lens of low self-esteem.

We are more likely to compare those areas of life in which others seem to be thriving while we are simply surviving – to hold up someone else's front-of-house next to our own behind-the-scenes. In recent years, the increased use of social media means we are privy to hundreds of thousands of personal images every day, feeding us constant fodder for comparison. Of course, we can rationalise to ourselves that what we see is never the complete picture, and that even an unfiltered photograph is merely a snapshot of a bigger scene we haven't witnessed. However, it's harder to encourage ourselves to see others in a realistic light when we view ourselves through the misty lens of low self-esteem. Our comparison becomes harsher and less favourable.

The great thing is that as we become more accepting of our flawed human selves, we are less likely to lend such weight and power to the snapshots we see of other people's lives.

You tell yourself how to feel

My partner left me when I was eight weeks pregnant with my first child. Every time I felt sad, I told myself to look on the bright side. My friend's husband left her with three kids. Her situation was worse.

Anonymous

Here's a different kind of comparison that we all engage in, yet we often don't realise it! Once you know what emotional comparison is, you'll start to notice yourself and others doing it all the time. It's those moments where you compare your feelings to someone else's situation, and decide that you 'shouldn't' be feeling like you do, or you try to change what you feel. Here are some examples of the sort of things we tell ourselves:

- I shouldn't be stressed, because other people have it harder.
- Look on the bright side, I'm so lucky.
- Buck up – they're dealing with it so much better than I am.
- I shouldn't feel overwhelmed! I don't have as much on my plate as my friend does.

Feelings are feelings, not facts. When you compare your emotions to someone else's situation, you are shaming your very valid response to what you're feeling. Feelings are feelings, not facts, and it's impossible to compare one to the other. Emotions are transient: they come and go like waves. When you tell yourself that you 'shouldn't feel like this', you halt the natural movement of the emotion and replace it with criticism, shame and frustration, directed towards yourself.

When I was younger, my sister sadly died of cancer. I lost count of the times friends said to me, 'Oh, I can't complain, because you lost your sister.' Yes, I did lose her. But does that mean none of my friends deserved to feel grief at the loss of a pet or a grandparent? Human emotion is not ranked in a hierarchy according to who deserves to feel what. There will always be someone who has had it harder or easier than you do, but someone else's broken leg doesn't make your stubbed toe hurt any less, just like someone else's hardship doesn't make yours feel easier to bear.

Of course, awareness of other people's circumstances can help you feel grateful for yours. But use that gratitude to bring balance. You can feel overwhelmed *and* grateful at the same time. The gratitude doesn't make the sense of overwhelm invalid. We don't rush to compare happiness, do we? *I shouldn't feel happy about my new job because someone else is getting married!* Allowing yourself to feel your feelings is a statement of worth.

You find it hard to accept kindness from others

When someone compliments me, it makes me want to disappear into the ground.

Lena

An act of kindness is a statement of value. Whether it takes the form of a gift, a compliment, a listening ear, or an act of generosity, the kindness of others can be hard to receive when your self-esteem is low. You may feel undeserving of it.

When I was at school, we'd sit in a circle to celebrate a friend's birthday and take it in turns to present our gifts. I remember being the birthday girl and feeling deeply uneasy at the attention and the parcels. I also remember feeling the same during a massage I once received as a Christmas present. I felt so unworthy of the masseuse's time (even though she had been paid) that I spent the whole time asking her questions about her life, in the hope that I was somehow giving something back to her.

Low self-esteem often has us feeling undeserving and tempted to over-repay acts of kindness. If you rate your worth at 2/10 and someone treats you like you're worth 10/10, the discrepancy is uncomfortable. It feels like a debt that needs to be repaid somehow.

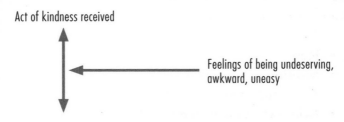

Act of kindness received

Feelings of being undeserving, awkward, uneasy

What you believe you're worth

The more you recognise the truth – that you are worthy of kindness – the smaller that uncomfortable gap becomes.

You sometimes feel burnt out

I fill up my diary, saying yes to everything, and then I fall into an exhausted heap at the weekend and feel like hiding under the covers because I'm all empty.

Sonia

Imagine if all of your resources had a financial cost attached to them:

- Having friends round   = 10 coins
- Cooking dinner   = 2 coins
- Comforting a friend   = 3 coins
- Keeping the house tidy = 4 coins

You have a limited number of coins to spend each day and once they're gone, they're gone. But the good thing is that there are many ways in which you can earn more coins. Some examples include:

- Rest
- Meeting your needs
- Accepting support
- Acknowledging feelings
- Spending time outside
- Doing things that bring you happiness

However, if you keep spending without earning, you end up in debt. You are running on empty. You are giving what you don't have – and that's expensive. Your diary might be full but if your resources are low or depleted, you can end up feeling burnt out, exhausted and wanting to retreat. You become resentful and, quite frankly, fed up.

If you find yourself seeking a sense of worth from doing, you're far more likely to end up on the burnout roller-coaster – giving and crashing, giving and crashing. But as you work on self-esteem and develop more respect for the fact that your resources have a cost attached to them, you can become more mindful of how you spend them and top them up.

You find it challenging to assert boundaries

I hate it when people shorten my name, but I never ask them to stop. I don't want it to be awkward or make them feel guilty.

Lauren

Your boundaries are defined by those actions and behaviours that enforce your beliefs. They let the people around you know how you like to be treated. Boundaries also communicate how you treat others and how you prefer to react in different situations. Where you choose to place your boundaries is shaped by your experience, culture and many other factors along the way. For example, I don't like to swear in front of my children and I hold that boundary by not swearing in front of them. Should a friend repeatedly swear within earshot of them, I might enforce my boundary by asking my friend if she could be aware of her language around my kids. If I didn't want to enforce the boundary because I feared offending my friend or making things awkward, I'd avoid saying anything. Internally, though, I might feel uncomfortable and irritated. Perhaps next time, I'd invite her round when my kids weren't there.

I find that the lower my self-esteem is, the harder it is for me to assert my boundaries, because I end up seeking validation from others and don't want to do anything to risk them liking me less. Yet when I let others push through or mow down my boundaries, I feel hurt, resentful and walked over. Often, they have no idea they've overstepped my boundaries at all!

When your self-esteem is low, it's common to value the comfort, needs and feelings of others over your own. It can feel awkward or intimidating to assert the fact that something is uncomfortable or hurtful for you. As you learn to value and validate your own feelings and needs, you will find more confidence in affirming them and be less fearful of the repercussions of doing so.

You don't like to ask for support

Things have to be pretty bad before I ask for help. I can't stand being seen as needy.

Deana

Low self-esteem can have you plodding on alone, shrugging off any offers of support because of your fear of being a burden. On the off-chance that you do accept support or open up to someone, you can be hit with feelings of vulnerability and regret afterwards.

This is a biggie for me, as it's something I often struggle with and have to keep tabs on. The less I value myself, the less I deem myself worthy of asking for or accepting the sort of support that I so freely offer to others. I've always been very self-sufficient, desperate to meet my own needs so that I can avoid asking for help. Needing others has seemed like a failing, and when I've been supported or cared for, it's felt like the uncomfortable gift of that massage, which I thought I didn't deserve. My ultimate fear has been to be a burden to another person.

As you work on your self-esteem, you start to realise that you are in fact worthy of the support and kindness you offer others. You are not made to struggle on alone.

You engage in self-destructive behaviour

It became a running joke that all my relationships lasted nine months. Things would be getting serious so I'd throw a grenade in.

Normally I'd cheat or suddenly stop responding to contact. Therapy has helped me realise it all came down to not feeling worthy of love. This is the first time I've been in a relationship for over a year!

Nushka

If you don't believe you're worthy of good things and healthy relationships, you may find yourself sabotaging them. Self-sabotage manifests in different ways, from the obvious to the nuanced – from not drinking enough water, to procrastinating and ending up late for an important job interview, to pushing people away if you feel unworthy of enjoying friendship or connection.

I broke up with my boyfriend (now husband) multiple times in the first year of our relationship. I found it very hard to believe that he actually wanted to be with me, so I thought it best to end the relationship before he realised I wasn't good enough for him. This behaviour is self-punishing, as it can involve pushing away things that are beneficial, healthy or joy-bringing. The more you realise you're worthy of your happiness, the less likely you are to sabotage it.

You feel like an imposter

After my promotion at work I was on edge for months. I worried they'd realise they'd made a mistake.

Farouk

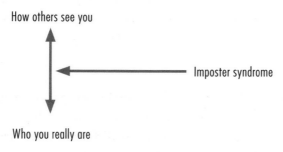

How others see you

Imposter syndrome

Who you really are

Imposter syndrome fills the gap between how you present yourself to the world and who you believe you really are underneath that facade. You might be given a promotion at work and you know that your boss must think you're capable of the increased responsibility. Yet you feel like an imposter, waiting for your boss or team to find out that it's all an act and you never deserved the recognition.

Maybe you feel like those around you are responding to a version of you that doesn't feel entirely authentic, and that your relationships are at risk because people don't know the 'real' you. Imposter syndrome is experienced by people in every single role and job. Some individuals may be entirely successful by the world's standards, yet they will still admit to experiencing imposter syndrome.

Imposter syndrome keeps us playing small and safe. Perhaps you don't believe that the 'real' you is good enough for the job or relationship you want. Perhaps you conclude that the good things in your life have come about through luck or accident, rather than acknowledging the significant part that you have played in your own success. The good news is that as our self-esteem increases, so does our confidence in being more honest with people and owning our strengths.

You experience feelings of depression or anxiety

My low self-esteem fed my depression and my depression fed my low self-esteem. It felt like an endless cycle.

Anonymous

If you struggle over whether you are worthy of being supported and having your feelings and needs validated by others, you're less likely to receive the support you deserve. Feeling unworthy also taints the good things in life, making them harder to enjoy. Good experiences and relationships make life rich and bring balance to the hard times; and when we find it difficult to accept and enjoy those good things, the hard and sad experiences seem amplified.

There have been extended periods of time in my own life when I've felt low or depressed.

When we see how costly something has been for us, it gives us the motivation to change.

It has felt like an oppressive, grey cloud has encompassed me, smothering my energy, dulling the sparkle in my eyes and removing the spring from my step. During those times, it becomes harder to summon the energy required to rationalise anxious or intrusive thoughts, or to coach myself through waves of social anxiety or the drive to please others. When those emotions and behaviours go unchecked for a while, I find myself on a downward spiral. Slowly the things that make me feel worthy of the good stuff in life are nudged out of my days and my diary. Into the void floods self-doubt, self-criticism, self-sabotage and an overwhelming sense of unworthiness. That grey cloud distorts my vision of the sunny things in my life and prevents me from feeling their warmth.

What I have learnt over the years is that even when my self-esteem has dropped into muddy ground, and the lens through which I see the world is blurred, there always remains a glimmer of hope that I will feel the warmth of sunshine again. It sure takes a lot of energy to turn things round, but I now know how to shift that downward spiral into an upward direction. For me, this includes positive self-talk, rest and chatting honestly with those around me, asking for their support. This book is your map of ways to help yourself feel the heat of the sunshine again too.

To sum up

Everything has a cost. Everything we give of ourselves has a cost, and when we give relentlessly yet don't believe we are worthy of receiving and resting, our self-esteem will continue on a downward spiral. I hope this chapter has helped you see the cost that low self-esteem has had for you. You've given and given, yet this has not given you what you've needed to receive in return: a sense of your self-worth and how you are worthy of being loved, liked and able to enjoy the good things in

life. There is a cost for low self-esteem, and you
have paid that price.

Yet there is so much hope, I promise. When we
truly see how costly something has been for us, it
gives us the motivation to change it. I have written
this book in the hope that I can encourage you and
help you make the changes you need to make.

JOURNAL POINTS

- How might things look different if you
  respected and valued yourself more?
- Which of the characteristics of low self-esteem
  resonated the most with you?
- What have three of the main costs of low self-
  esteem been for you?
- How do you feel about accepting support
  from others?
- Do you rest enough? If not, what stops you?

Chapter 2

What's your story?

Mantra: *My past shapes me but doesn't define me.*

How you experienced life in your younger years sets the tone for how you perceive your self-worth in adulthood. In this chapter, I am going to list some of the common narratives you may have picked up during childhood and shine a light on them to bring them into focus. In therapy, it can be an absolute game-changer when we start to make the connections between the dynamics of family life and the way we relate to ourselves. It helps us separate out our true worth from the things that may have had us questioning it.

How we are wired

Imagine building your own home from scratch on a budget. You use the skills you have learnt in life. Every now and again, you ask a friend to come over and help you tile a floor or paint a wall. You wire the house by following online tutorials – and now a tangle of wires lies hidden behind the plastered walls. As the years pass, the flaws begin to show. The toaster blows a fuse, the bedroom door creaks, tiles sporadically fall off the walls and shatter, and the hob sparks. You did the best job you could with the knowledge and support you had at the time, with varying degrees of success. This self-built house is a metaphor for parenting. Parents tend to do the best they can with the resources, knowledge and support they have available to them at the time.

There is no such thing as the perfect parent.

My parents did the best job they could, too. They used their tools and knowledge, although there were no online tutorials and podcasts back then! Sure, the building of me was a bit flawed, because they, as the builders, were flawed. But aren't we all? There is no such thing as the perfect parent. (Although I spent my first few years of motherhood berating myself for not being one!) As the years passed, the cracks start to show. Every now and again, my internal wiring sparks and needs attention; my foundations crumble a little and need reinforcing. I've found it incredibly helpful to become aware of how my understanding of my worth has been shaped throughout my life, starting in childhood. This insight gives me the opportunity to address any issues proactively, be it an unhelpful thought pattern or a habit. If I don't act, those cracks will continue to grow and the gaps in my foundations will become that little bit wider with time.

If you had a very happy childhood, perhaps this chapter won't resonate with you as much as it will for other people.

If that's the case, we will be touching on some of the wider influences on self-esteem in the next chapter.

This is no blame game

I've sat with many clients over the years who've been worried that looking back at their childhood would mean betraying their caregivers. As we've seen, the truth is that the majority of our caregivers did the best parenting they could with the knowledge, resources and support that were available to them. We are all flawed, bringing our own histories and experiences to every circumstance. We all learn along the way in life.

Many parents look back and, in retrospect, wish they had done certain things differently – as do I. Through parenting my own young children, I can see how the experience and insights I've gained over the past few years will continue to shape how I relate and respond to them in the future. While we cannot change the past, we can make amends and access resources to improve the way we relate to ourselves and others in the years ahead.

If your caregivers have intentionally or unintentionally hurt or abused you, or betrayed your vulnerability, it can be very beneficial to seek counselling. Please turn to Helpful Contacts, page 265, for more information.

Challenging what we have learnt

*I thought I would spend my life scared about what others thought.
But when I look over the last year, I can see how my confidence
has grown.*

Fi

Do you know what I love most about being a therapist? It's
the hope. No matter what our histories and experiences
are, how low we feel, or how floor-skimming and low our
confidence is, there is hope. With the right insight and
support, things do shift and change. We can rewire homes,
we can dig up and rejig foundations, we can upgrade glasses
prescriptions. Your worth doesn't change, but your understanding of it can: we can challenge what we've come to
believe about ourselves.

**Becoming aware of
something gives us the
power to change it.**

I'm going to share with you
some of the most common messages we receive about ourselves
in childhood. They shape our
understanding of where to turn and
what to do in order to feel acceptable and good enough for
the world around us. At the end of each message, you'll find
a brief insight into how the family dynamic or behaviour
you experienced was quite likely originally motivated by a
good intention. Recognising these messages and patterns
doesn't need to involve apportioning blame, but allows
us to choose to model different behaviours and ways of
being. Becoming aware of something gives us the power
to change it.

You are what you do

My nan brought me up. I don't remember her sitting down. She was always busy and I realised I was the same at home too.

Anonymous

My mum shouldered many responsibilities. She was the breadwinner, the family chauffeur, the comforter, the diary manager, the housekeeper, the argument negotiator. She was many things to many different people, and everything to us. As a child, learning from what I saw, I believed that to be an acceptable and valid person, you should always be busy doing things for others and giving of yourself. You gave regardless of your energy levels and resources. Like me, my mum (a fellow therapist!) has recognised how her own lovely mother modelled this behaviour to her. These ways of being are often generational, because we learn how to be an adult through watching those with whom we grow up.

After working on my self-esteem in recent years, I'm more aware of the fact that my worth isn't dictated by how much I give and do. This enables me to choose to model something different to my own children. I want them to see me rest so that they know they deserve relaxation too. I want them to witness me asserting boundaries to prevent burnout, so that they know they don't need to work their way to worth either.

Good intention: caregivers model 'doing' because that's how they show love. It can often be sacrificial, because they may have learnt during their own childhood that giving of yourself makes you a good person.

You are what you look like

Everyone used to say my younger sister was beautiful. They never said it to me. I grew up feeling like the ugly sister. I never brought boyfriends home because I assumed they'd want to be with her instead. No matter how much my husband tells me he's attracted to me, I find it hard to believe.

Anonymous

When a friend sends me a new baby photo, my immediate response is to say how beautiful their baby is. From a young age, our appearance is remarked upon, teaching us that it must be of great importance. This message is powerful and shapes our understanding of what makes us acceptable. Airbrushing, diet culture and social-media filters have fed the belief that there is an ideal way to look if we wish to be acceptable and worthy of success.

One person does not have more worth than another person simply because of the way they look. It's a truth that we often have to keep reminding ourselves of. I remind myself of it as I catch myself eyeing up the bathroom scales. I notice how differently I feel about myself depending on the number of kilos displayed. Perhaps I sashay out of the house and stand a little taller, or I may grab an oversized jumper and berate myself instead. People may treat me or view me differently depending on whether I'm dressed up or sporting unwashed hair, hormonal acne and breakfast-spattered leggings. But that is probably because they are seeing me through the same lens that I am. We have to work extra hard to address unhelpful habits when we are constantly having to navigate our way through a culture that reinforces them.

Good intention: a caregiver may treat us in particular ways, depending on their own wish to adhere to certain social expectations. Maybe you witnessed them diet or become fixated on certain aspects of appearance. They may even have tried to influence your own appearance in an attempt to protect you from judgement.

You are defined by how efficient you are

Once, I got a stomach bug and couldn't leave my room for three days. I don't want to sound dramatic, but it actually gave me a kind of identity crisis.

Taya

The other day, my husband did a high-intensity workout session in our bedroom. My eyes skimmed the room, the unmade bed and pile of washing on the floor. I asked him what he'd been doing during the session's rest periods. 'Erm, resting?' he replied.

My sense of worth is tied up in what and how much I do – to the extent that I couldn't comprehend resting during workout breaks. I'd use each twenty-second 'rest' to shove a jumper in the wardrobe or a pillow on the bed. For me, being efficient feeds my self-esteem; or it does for a while at least, until I'm shattered, or something prevents me from doing everything as quickly as I'd like. Then my self-esteem takes a dive and I feel like a failure.

Good intention: a caregiver may shun their own rest because they value efficiency and other people's comfort more than their own needs.

You are how clever you are

At primary school, I got six out of ten in my spelling test and I was terrified to tell Dad. He always quizzed me about the stuff I got wrong. He died ten years ago. Even now, I feel fear whenever I get feedback at work.

Leona

If you receive praise and attention only when you do well, you may form the belief that doing well is what makes you lovable and acceptable.

My brother found it easier to get good school grades than I did. I'd sit and study at my desk for hours, surrounded by neon sticky notes. Even though I never felt pressured to succeed academically, to me, our different abilities to retain information seemed indicative of my own failings. I found myself trying to prove that I could get good grades too. I even held my breath when getting the grade for my master's degree in my late twenties, wondering whether I had matched or bettered his grade!

Good intention: a caregiver may focus on achievement because they want you to have the career opportunities that come with good academic grades or more financial security for your future.

You are how kind you are

My mum would drop everything for anyone. She never said no to anything anyone asked her to do. It was tough for me to learn to say no, as it wasn't in my vocabulary.

Anonymous

As a child, I remember my mother saying, 'If you come to choosing a partner, always look for kindness.' Kindness is such a wonderful quality. We naturally gravitate towards kind people because we are more

Kindness without healthy boundaries is people-pleasing.

likely to be treated with respect. The challenge arises when being 'kind' comes with a big cost to the giver. Kindness without healthy boundaries is people-pleasing. If this is the type of kindness that has been modelled to us in childhood, it's likely that we will find ourselves displaying it too.

Another reason you may develop a strong need to please others is if your caregiver looked to you to meet a need of their own. Perhaps they looked to you in order to feel needed, praised or comforted themselves. Maybe they confided in you. Some children end up more or less parenting their own parents and attempting to meet their needs as a way to keep them happy.

Good intention: kindness is praised, yet there is often a hidden cost. It seems to go hand in hand with being a 'good person', but if you've not been taught to place boundaries around your resources, then it is hard to model boundaries to children. Moreover, if your parent has looked to you to meet a need of their own, the reasons for your people-pleasing are rarely conscious.

You are as straightforward as you are

My dad was an alcoholic. There was enough drama. I kept everything in my head because I wanted life to be easy.

Anonymous

Where you fit into the family dynamic shapes your self-identity. When my sister died, I found it hard to see my parents being upset. I didn't want to cause them even more stress, so I internalised feelings that would have been healthier to talk through. This became the way I approached struggles for many years to come.

> **Where you fit into the family dynamic shapes your self-identity.**

Although I gave the impression that I was 'okay', I was hiding my emotions and would often feel alone and misunderstood. I felt stuck between a rock and a hard place. I didn't know how else to be, although I did eventually discover another way – as you will too, in these pages. Finding the confidence to be honest about my internal world has been so important for me.

So much goes unsaid and uncomforted when you grow

up feeling like you need to be emotionally 'neat and tidy' and avoid potentially adding to or creating drama. Keeping your feelings locked away can easily become a habit.

Good intention: life's challenges, curveballs and traumas take up a lot of attention and emotional energy. Trying to be straightforward and 'not wanting to cause a fuss' can be aimed at restoring a healthy family dynamic, but because the family focus is often on the person who is overtly struggling, those members who seem okay but who are secretly struggling may slip under the radar.

You are the job you do

> *Both of my parents are teachers and I became one too. I find myself questioning whether I ever thought to be anything else.*

Priyanka

A dressing-up box sits in our playroom, which is overflowing with plastic stethoscopes, dolls and cowboy hats. When we ask kids what they want to be when they are older, we are ushering them towards the future and asking them to cast their minds decades ahead. As children, we likewise learnt that we were meant to become something when we were older – to play a role, have a job, go to work.

Over the last few years, I've tried hard not to ask, 'What do you do?' the first time I meet someone. It can be interesting to question why we like to know this about people . . . Is it because we are simply interested in how they spend their time? Or is it because we want know how we compare to them? I have worked in many roles over the years and have found myself answering the 'What do you do?' question with varying degrees of trepidation, aware that everyone draws their own assumptions. I've been a pub washer-upper, a switchboard operator, a sink plug maker, a barmaid, and many other jobs along the way. I've found myself qualifying some of my roles: 'Oh, I'm *just* a mum' or 'I'm *just* doing this while I study.'

The more your self-esteem is attached to what you do, the more you will fear the opinions of others or require their validation. The thing to remember is that everyone's opinions are unique and dependent on their own personal experiences, histories and world views. Someone else's opinion is absolutely not a statement of your validity.

Good intention: caregivers may have encouraged a child down a certain path in the hope that this will give them security, direction and a happy future. Perhaps they enjoyed having a particular career or wish they'd considered it – so hoped for the same thing for you.

You are what other people think about you

Mum and Dad would run around tidying before anyone came. They'd put on different voices. I'm the same, though; I literally feel like I'm being my mum sometimes.

Karen

If you grew up with caregivers who were quite concerned about the opinions of others, you may be preoccupied with similar thoughts. You might have interpreted this to mean that what others think of you is more important than just being yourself.

Perhaps your caregivers spent a lot of time talking about others, causing you to assume that others would be speaking about you in turn. Of course, we only ever see a snapshot of other people's lives, but it's a major thing to let the snapshot assumptions of others dictate whether or not you allow yourself to be yourself. (We will discuss this in more detail in chapter 9, on people-pleasing.)

Good intention: often people-pleasing behaviour manifests itself in a preoccupation with what others think, and then behaving in ways intended to please.

You are as strong you are

My grandad always told me to smile, not to cry. Sometimes I just wanted to feel sad for a minute.

Viv

It's not that strength and bravery aren't good. The challenge comes when very valid feelings are dismissed in our attempt to be strong. Perhaps you grew up in an environment where only certain emotions were well received and communicated. Perhaps you were told to 'smile, be happy and look on the bright side'. These words often come out of a loving place! It's hard to see someone we care about struggle, but it's good to validate the emotions they are feeling, rather than trying to change or fix them.

Imagine talking to someone who's been to a certain place in Devon. As they talk about a particular beach that you've visited as well, you are filled with memories – it's as if you were there yesterday. Likewise, a whiff of perfume or a particular soundtrack can conjure up a strong memory. The same thing can happen with our feelings. Someone speaking of their loss might remind you of your own sadness, while someone who is roaring with laughter can bring a smile to your face. Emotion in one person touches emotion in another.

A person might be tempted to try to help us, instead of listen to us, because what we are sharing with them causes them to think about their own emotions or experiences, which can be uncomfortable. Fixing, or asking others to adopt a positive mental attitude, is a way of trying to relieve another person of a feeling so that neither of you have to dwell on it. I notice when I do this too: I want to help someone feel better about their challenge or sadness so that I can feel better and more hopeful about mine.

The more you realise that you are worthy of feeling your feelings and of being heard, the more you are able to let the waves of emotion come and go, and to validate them regardless of how anyone else might respond to them.

Good intention: caregivers often encourage strength and bravery in the hope of making you feel better, or in an attempt to protect you or themselves from difficult emotions. Can you see how easily this approach becomes generational?

You are the stuff you possess

Our family kept getting into debt, trying to keep up with what everyone else was doing. They wanted people to think they were successful and that's what they felt they had to do.

Anonymous

As a child, I remember the constant adverts that punctuated the television programmes we watched. These days, adverts come at us in far more frequent and clever formats. I remember wanting to go to a friend's house because he had a ride-on train that chugged along a track – but it soon became clear that my siblings and I couldn't have what others had. It set us apart. We felt different, dressed in our second-hand school uniforms while other children wore crisp white shirts fresh from the packet. The cool kids at school seemed to be the ones with the cool things. And thus begins the early introduction of the message: 'you are what you have'.

Cognitively, we know that someone's worth isn't dictated by what they own. But our economy thrives on people upgrading, updating, slapping it on a credit card. No amount of stuff will ever remedy low self-esteem. It may provide a temporary boost in confidence, but it will not satisfy us in the long term.

Good intention: a need to 'have more' often comes from a desire to seek and provide happiness and good experiences.

You are how people describe you

My primary school teacher used to call me a stupid child. I didn't try hard at school because what was the point? My aunt helped me prepare for a maths test and we discovered I was good at maths! For the first time, I questioned what he'd said.

Anonymous

Consider how you were described in childhood. Were you the funny one, the quiet one, the tricky one, the bad sleeper, the fussy eater? Who were you told you were? I was the caring, creative one, while my brother was the quiet, clever one. My sister was the funny, wild one. Today, I notice myself doing the same thing when I describe my children to others. We all have a tendency to typecast each other in order to orientate people in our minds. We distil the complexity of another human being down into a few words.

How we were labelled in childhood can inform how we see ourselves, the decisions we make and the opportunities we seek in later life. I wonder what labels you were given along the way – as a toddler, as you played with friends, as you sat at your first school desk. What words always cropped up in your school reports? How did you overhear yourself being described by friends and family? We can easily go through life without questioning those labels, so ask yourself now whether you liked being described that way. Does it feel in line with how you see yourself?

As a child, you probably looked to your caregiver to tell you how to view yourself and the world. If they appeared to think something was safe, you'd have felt more confident in approaching it. If something consistently angered them, you might have approached it with trepidation. If they told you that you were tricky, you were unlikely to question this for a good few years, until you were old enough to gain a wider understanding of how people see you.

Instead of viewing these labels as opinions, you may have formed statements about yourself based upon the things that other people said: 'my parents thought I was the difficult one!' turns into 'I was a difficult child'. In this way, an opinion becomes a statement. It's such a valuable exercise to note which labels you've been wearing all your life, and to call them to question!

Good intention: a description of you may have tripped off the tongue during a tense moment, or have been offered in a fond or humorous way without the intention of hurting you. Perhaps in some instances, things were said without you understanding the wider context.

You are how well you are loved

Mum never once hugged me. I thought she didn't love me. Years on, she told me that her dad used to treat her badly. It's been hard trying to think differently, but we talk about it which helps me understand.

Anonymous

As small children, we are egocentric. Meaning, we think everything that everyone else does is somehow because of us. If someone is kind to you, you think you are good; if someone is cruel, it's because you are bad. If you overhear your parents fighting, you assume it must be because of something you've done wrong.

If you were neglected in some way – not often listened to or comforted – then you may find it hard to validate and comfort yourself as an adult. If you were bullied, you may continue to bully yourself internally, in the way you speak to and treat yourself.

Good intention: the main reason caregivers aren't able to communicate love well is because they lacked a healthy model and experience of how to love and communicate love.

To sum up

Few people set out to be a less-than-good-enough parent or caregiver. It's hard to give what one does not have. But whilst some behaviour may be explained, it doesn't mean it always needs to be excused. Being able to explain or understand someone's hurtful or destructive treatment of you doesn't mean you don't have a right to mourn what wasn't, or give space to the very valid feelings you have.

If you were presented with a skewed perception of what makes you worthy of the good things in life, it's understandable that your self-esteem has been skewed too. The overwhelmingly positive thing is that our generation has more tools and insights available to it than ever before – both for gaining clarity about why we are the way we are, and for strengthening our self-esteem and confidence. I have found it extremely helpful to access these

What you've been through shapes who you are, but it doesn't need to define you.

readily available tools, knowledge and support to ensure that I am parenting with all those considerations in mind.

You can change your self-esteem. What you've been through shapes who you are, but it doesn't need to define you. Regardless of how you were loved, or not, you can learn to accept and respect yourself beyond what you were taught. It's hard work sometimes, but I can assure you it's possible, life-changing and worthwhile. If you think you'd benefit from extra help to separate out what you've been taught about yourself from your real, inherent worth, therapeutic support can help (see Helpful Contacts, page 265).

JOURNAL POINTS

- Which of the common childhood messages, listed above, resonated the most for you?
- How has your self-esteem been impacted by these messages?
- How might you be continuing to play out those childhood messages in your behaviour today?

- What new messages might you like to replace them with?
- Would you benefit from some extra insight to help you separate out learnt messages from your inner truth?

Chapter 3

Buy now, pay later

*Mantra: Making a good decision for myself
is an act of worth.*

Now we've taken time to explore how our self-esteem
is shaped within our family setting, we're going to head
beyond the front door to see how the wider world and
culture impact self-esteem too! Like all of us, my own
understanding of the world began at home. However, once
I ventured beyond those first formative years, I began to
form my own world view and perceive things through the
lenses of my own understanding. We are more exposed to
the wider world around us than ever before, so exploring its
influence on us is important. The better we understand our
relationship with the world, the less passive we will be in
response to the ways in which it impacts our understanding
of our self-worth.

Two self-esteem sources

I feel the hunger pang rising in my stomach after a morning of work. I have two options! My first option is to grab the bag of sweets sitting temptingly beside me. Not only will they silence the growl in my belly, but they'll provide a glorious, short, sharp sugar boost. Option two is to leave my desk to make a plate of roast chicken leftovers and a baked potato. It requires more effort, but would fill me up for a few hours. Slow and steady.

We face these types of decisions all the time. Do we do something we know will be good for us, but requires more energy and input, or do we find a way to quickly meet or silence the need momentarily? My clients spend a lot of time with me exploring where they go to get a feeling of good self-esteem. Where you go looking for validation has a huge impact on whether you find it or not, and how long it lasts before you need a top-up.

When it comes to raising our self-esteem, a boost can come from two types of sources:

1. Short and sharp self-esteem boosters
2. Slow and steady self-esteem boosters

Let's explore these two self-esteem boosting sources in more detail.

Short and sharp self-esteem boosters

*Sometimes I just want to do what makes me feel better NOW, even
if I know I'll probably regret it later on.*

Frankie

Short and sharp self-esteem boosters are like that bag of
sweets or a hastily grabbed, salty takeaway burger. They
promise a quick and easy way to meet a need, but often
they end up being temporary fixes instead. For me, they
are those impulse buys that made me feel good – and then
guilty. They are the text message I send in place of having
a chat. They are the slapdash job I do to save time and then
have to redo later. They are the words of flattery I offer to
make someone feel good, in the hope they'll like me. They
are the times I give resources I don't have in order to please
others, which I later resent. They are the moments of digital escapism that distract me from
finding the good in the challenges of the present moment.
They are the chaotic working
hours that sabotage my sleep.

**Short, sharp self-esteem
boosters often conflict with
our personal values.**

These short, sharp self-esteem
boosters often conflict with our personal values. For example, I know that it's the feedback from those who know
me well that matters the most, yet part of me still seeks
affirmation from strangers on social media. The issue is, we
need endless short and sharp self-esteem boosters if we are
hooked on their immediacy; yet their short, sharp sweetness
will never truly satisfy us.

Slow and steady self-esteem boosters

I always used to paint but life just got busy. I started again recently and remembered why I used to love it. It gives me so much.

Lorna

These are the nourishing self–esteem boosters. If they were a food, they'd be the lovingly prepared food eaten in good company. They are the things that ground and anchor you, and bring you joy and meaning. They are the creative pursuits, the acts that bring you back to yourself and make you feel grateful and present. They are the things that, when you are grey and old, you'll wish with all your heart you'd spent time doing more often.

For me, they are being with my kids without the background ping of a phone. They are walking through pine forests, the tall trees stretching towards moody skies. They are laughter that makes my sides ache. They are the hot bath that warms cold bones. They are the dinners shared around a table where the food is good but the company is better. They are the times I apologise and feel forgiveness. I could go on ... Once you begin writing down the things that make your life feel worthwhile, you'll also start to get into the flow!

These slow and steady boosters help us connect with who we are and what we are worth. They don't necessarily offer us quick spikes of energy, but a warm, slow burn. They sometimes require more planning, but are worth it as they bring feelings of joy, identity, gratitude and fulfilment. Many of these slow and steady self–esteem boosters have no goals other than to offer us connection and wellbeing.

Finding the balance

My boyfriend is always complaining that I have my head in work even when I'm not at the office. I feel like the years are slipping away. We want kids at some point, but I keep putting off the conversation. We had a proper chat about it. We agreed I'd talk to my colleague about handing some projects over. Something needs to change.

Anonymous

Oh, balance! We all seek the things that make us feel better about ourselves. But life today is an ongoing juggle between knowing what we need, and being told what we want! I know I need to feel properly connected to my support network, yet my phone tells me I can achieve this via a quick message. Sometimes a quick text message exchange does the trick, but ultimately it will never provide the quality of connection offered by a proper catch-up over coffee. It's all about trying to seek balance between getting what we need and what we can get *now*.

Balance is one of those things that we rarely find (and if we do, it's not often for long, hey?), but which is very good to seek. In seeking balance, we are more likely to move away from destructive or consuming behaviours that do not satisfy us. Life is really lived in the grey after all. Here's a quick example: imagine you're juggling home and work life ...

- You want to please your boss = short and sharp self-esteem boost.
- You want to invest in some drifting friendships = slow and steady self-esteem boost.

Herein lies the challenge: if you prioritise your drifting friendships, and ignore the pressure to please your boss by taking on more responsibility and overtime, your boss may be displeased. Yet if you accept every single extra hour of overtime, spending longer at your desk to show willing and please your boss, you'll lose out on investing in those relationships that give you something important. Sometimes the pull in one direction is stronger than the other, and sometimes we successfully navigate a tightrope dance between the two.

There is nothing wrong with getting your hits from the short and sharp self-esteem boosters sometimes, but if they are the main ways you seek feelings of worth, your self-esteem will rise and fall as the hit wears off. Just like if you fuelled your body with a diet of sweets, you'd be riding the peaks and troughs of sugar hits. You wouldn't be respectfully providing your body with the nutrition it needs to sustain you for work and rest – just superficial, temporary highs.

Know your personal values

Now we've taken a moment to look at these two internal and external sources of self-esteem, let's explore how your personal values impact how you feel about your-

Your personal values reflect the things that are important to you.

self. Your personal values reflect the things that are important to you, what you stand for and the kind of person you are. They are influenced by your experience of family, culture and faith, and both your internal and external life experiences. Some of your values will be fixed, while others will have been added as you navigated the different challenges in your life so far. Here are some examples of values:

- Friendship is important to me.
- I support the beliefs of that politician.
- I will fight for environmental rights.
- I don't like lying.
- Family should support each other.
- It's not okay to abuse anyone.
- Football is important for community morale.
- I don't want to parent like my mother.

Perhaps a few of the values that really used to matter to you, don't matter much anymore. Maybe some of the things you never gave a lot of thought to are now the things that shape your values. Many of your values have tangible labels, such as what political party you support, whether you cheer for a certain sports team, or follow a religion. Others are harder to define, but are felt when they are challenged, or a boundary has been pushed.

We have both positive and negative values. Some of my positive values are:

- I value quality time with family.
- My priority is to try to be present.
- It's important to keep in touch with people I care about.

- I like to exercise in a way that respects and strengthens my body.
- I want to aim for work–life balance.
- I don't like being late.
- I value honesty in myself and others.
- I don't like it when people have their voices taken away.

Your positive values are likely to be in line with the slow and steady self-esteem boosters you seek. They work well together and support each other. If every decision you made was in line with your positive values, and every self-esteem boost was of the slow and steady variety, you would hopefully feel a lot more fulfilled.

But we all pick up some negative values along the way too. These don't serve you as well, as they tend to be influenced by difficult and challenging life experiences, with the aim of protecting you from being hurt in some way. Whilst intending to protect you, they can also lower your self-esteem, because when you protect yourself from negative feelings and experiences, you're often also preventing yourself from fully engaging in the good ones. For example, if I build a high wall without a door around my home, sure, I won't get burgled, but nice visitors won't have access to me either!

Some of the negative core values that I have held include:

- To accept help is to fail.
- If I say no to others, they won't like me.
- If I'm honest about how I feel, people will reject me.

- Underneath it all, I'm not worthy of love.
- To rest is inefficient.
- Self-care is indulgent.
- My worth is based on what I do for others.

I've lived to the tune of these core values and I can tell you that rejecting help, always saying yes, never sharing my struggles and shying away from love because I didn't think I deserved it became the reason my self-esteem hovered around floor level. As I've become more visible, authentic and present in my own life, I've encountered opinions, judgements and those who've not appreciated my boundaries; but I've also encountered more connection and enjoyment. When they remain unchallenged, our negative values have a lot of power to inform the way we live. We will be focussing on and challenging these beliefs in the pages to come.

The tug of war

While you have your own personal values, these are influenced by the values of the culture and world around you. The values of society form a map of how to behave, how to be accepted, how to be successful and how not to end up in prison. They are sometimes contradictory and confusing, and about as clear as crystal, mud or somewhere in between. We are constantly assessing the value systems of the world, cultures and people around us, and whether they conflict with our own values, and whether or not we will adhere to them.

Here's another example. Let's say I need a clear weekend as life has been so busy and I feel the familiar sensation of burnout looming. I yearn to take the space to breathe and to have some family time before starting yet another busy work week. However, I receive a text message inviting me to an exhibition that a friend is featuring in. It means a lot to her that I go, but it would take up an entire day due to the long drive to get there. Let's look at all those contradictory thoughts that create that familiar feeling of 'eek, what do I do?'

- My personal positive value: *It's important to me to put boundaries in place to prevent burnout.*
- My personal negative value: *I can't say no because she'll think I don't care about her.*
- A cultural value: *You only live once! It will be fun!*
- Short and sharp self-esteem lift: *I'll go because then she'll be happy with me and that will feel good.*
- Slow and steady self-esteem lift: *I'll say, 'I can't this weekend, sorry', to make way for the slow weekend I need.*

Not too long ago, I'd have gone to the exhibition to please my friend. I'd have then spent the next week feeling tearful, tired and resentful that I never got an opportunity to rest. I'd be frustrated with myself for not being able to assert my boundaries and my self-respect would likely wobble, sending my self-esteem on a dip. It'd be the short-term gain of approval at the cost of the longer-term consequences that come from repeatedly valuing other people's feelings and needs over my own.

These days I'd say a very grateful, 'Sorry, I can't.' I'd

see whether my friend had any other exhibition dates, or whether we could meet up at a later time for her to show me some photos of her work. I might see if she could video-call me and show me around virtually. I'd try not to make insincere excuses for not going, but take the opportunity to be honest with her: 'I'm sad to miss out, but I've been running myself into the ground with work and just need a home-based weekend.' Perhaps she would be annoyed with me, triggering my shame and guilt and feeding that negative value of mine: 'I can't say no!' If so, I'd remind myself that I can't expect everyone to understand how I feel, or why I need to place my boundaries where I do. If she's a good friend, this should not impact our relationship.

> **If your self-esteem is low, you are more likely to compromise your own values.**

Now, the aim of this chapter isn't to give you a magic formula that will help you create a perfect balance between your own values and those of the world. It's simply to draw your attention to how many different things are pulling on who you are. If your self-esteem is low, you are more likely to repeatedly compromise your own values in order to please others. You might gain more acceptance from them, but it's a type of self-neglect. As your self-esteem increases, you will recognise that your needs and feelings are important. And as your confidence grows, you'll place more value on your own voice. What matters to you; what hurts you; what is respectful to you; what fulfils you; what makes you feel grounded and alive – those things are important. Very important.

The hunt for happy

If you ask someone what one thing they want for their life, or the lives of their loved ones, they often say 'happiness'. It's something we seek because it brings enjoyment. We are wired to hunt for happy. Happiness keeps us working, relating, moving around, motivated and active. I do so many things throughout the day with the aim of bringing about happiness later on. I tidy up and answer emails in order to relax when my kids go to bed. I spend time in front of the cooker so that we can sit and enjoy a nice meal. I work in the hope of earning a holiday at a later date. I keep in touch with friends so that I can enjoy the fruits of friendship. I wrestle the kids' limbs into coats because I know that the fresh air and woodland will bring us happiness when we go out.

Now think of a caveman: if he didn't feel gratified sitting around the campfire and enjoying that day's hunting catch, he would be less motivated to head out and do it again. Often happiness and enjoyment follow an investment of time, energy or resources. This is the natural order of things. Yet modern life turned that on its head by offering short-cuts – have the happiness now and pay later!

The problem is that today we're spoilt for choice, which means our desires tend to grow ever hungrier and bigger. Think of simple pleasures such as rocking in an old chair and thumbing the pages of a novel, or singing around a piano, or inhaling the musty air after a rainfall. In the modern world, these pleasures often sit in the shade of the thousands of other options for bigger, faster, 'better' happiness hits. We know these sorts of glamorous boosts can't satisfy us for long or our bank account will suffer. But we're repeatedly told this doesn't really matter and sign ourselves up all the same, while the small print detailing the hidden cost gets smaller and more complicated, hidden from view. It becomes harder to choose more nourishing choices. This is why it's important to strengthen our awareness of what is good for us, even if it doesn't offer an immediate boost. When we recognise the real self-esteem boosting statements of our worth, we'll be more likely to make different choices.

How do our choices relate to worth?

If you make the decision to do something that is good and nourishing for you, be that physically, emotionally or mentally, this is an act of worth. It is saying something validating to yourself.

Think of it this way: if every time my kids asked for food, I were to shove a handful of sweets at them, they might indeed be delighted, but I would be overlooking their need for real nourishment. It might seem more convenient to chuck them a snack than to make a sandwich; their requests would stop and I'd get a moment to sit down. But, in time, the novelty would wear off and they'd crave something more fulfilling.

If I continued to shovel sweets their way, I would not be valuing and respecting them in my actions. Their teeth would suffer, the level of their blood sugar would nosedive. What would my actions be telling them about how much I valued them? Actions say so much. I could tell them I love them 1,000 times a day, but if I'm not showing them love in the way I treat them and the boundaries I set in place on their behalf, my words would lose their clout. There are times for sweets, for sure! But sweets alone do not a nutritious diet make!

To sum up

Try to put aside the temptation to seek the perfect balance. Instead, just focus on becoming more sensitive to that still, small, quiet voice inside yourself that tells you how you feel in different circumstances. The one that tells you 'I don't like this' or 'that makes me feel uneasy'.

Start to look for the options that arise which perhaps you didn't realise were there before. Say, for example, I always used to say yes if someone asked me for something. It was my instant and habitual reaction because I didn't want them to think they couldn't rely on me. Now, instead, I would remind myself that there is another option available to me! I could say, 'I can't this time.' It sounds obvious, but without that self-awareness my need to help others and my fear of disappointing them would immediately override my own need for things such as personal space, downtime and support. This is about a process, a chipping away of those long-held habits that used to lead us to seek the quick self-esteem boost, or the easy option. It's not about getting anything 'right'; it's about becoming aware of our choices, not necessarily all the time, but more of the time.

JOURNAL POINTS

- Take a moment to note down some of your go-to 'slow and steady' self-esteem boosts and see how you feel as you do.
- Where in life have you been sacrificing the 'nourishing' for the 'right now'?
- List some of those negative values you've held. How does it feel to see them written down?
- Challenge each of those negative values and their validity as statements about who you are.
- Write down some value statements about the things that are important to you and the way you live. How might you bring some of your decisions more in line with them?

Chapter 4

Why in the world do we feel like this?

Mantra: *I control my self-esteem.*

Regardless of the nature of our upbringing, how validated we were by those who looked after us and how much we were loved, our self-esteem is still impacted by the world around us. This is the result of major influences, such as the law, politics and how our country deals with challenges and events, and more personal ones, such as the dynamics of friendship groups and office cultures.

The world is a loud place that is constantly pulling our attention in different directions. We are bombarded with adverts telling us what we want and how to spend our money. And then there is the symphony of 'pings' coming at us from our phones and laptops, telling us we're needed. It doesn't stop. I've never felt so connected to so many people, so much information and to so many different opinions and messages, yet I've never found it harder to be connected to myself – my opinions, my needs, my internal messages.

If you want to improve your self-esteem, notice what's jostling for the power to tell you who you are, how to live and what makes you acceptable. Then you can tweak your boundaries and relationship to those things, lessening the impact they have on you – and that's what we're going to do in this chapter. For those of us whose self-esteem had a bumpy start in life, there is so much hope, I promise.

Our phones

Sometimes I fantasise about the days when phones were attached to walls and when emails were only in a computer on your desk at work.

Karen

I had no idea about how much my phone had begun to impact my sense of worth until I recently put in place some serious boundaries around my phone usage. Did you ever hear the story about the frog in the pan of boiling water? I think (and hope) it's metaphorical, but it's a helpful tale for me. The story goes that if you plop a frog into a pan of boiling water, it will try to hop straight out, like my cat did when he fell into the bath recently. Gosh, the speed! However, if you put a frog into a pan of cold water, slowly nudging the temperature up, it will boil alive. I think this is what has happened for many of us with our phone use.

One of my internal values is that I don't want to spend too

much time on my phone, yet it's very hard not to. It contains my support network, my entertainment, my office, my life admin, my escapism and much more! No longer is it the norm to 'clock off' at a set time in the day. Work and home, social and family, inside world and outside world – they all merge and blur together, a cacophony of pings, swoops and dings calling our attention away from the present moment. They are little 'micro stressors' interrupting the flow of now. Sure, each bleep might not feel that stressful, but they certainly do add up.

I feel guilty when I'm 'just adding something to the shop' on my phone, whilst my kids repeatedly call my name. When I'm looking at my phone, I answer questions on autopilot, and recently I agreed to a request for a snack before dinner because I just wasn't listening. I've felt my stomach lurch because of a comment on a social-media feed in which I felt misunderstood, resulting in my family being robbed of my attention on a Sunday afternoon. Just knowing that my attention is drawn in so many directions contradicts my own values.

It takes effort to change a habit, but it's so much better in the long run if it means that your new boundaries spare you from some of those waves of guilt or frustration with yourself. If a twenty-minute, mindless scroll on your phone finds you tempted to compare yourself to others on social media, or angry with yourself because you were distracted when you really wanted to be more present, then your self-esteem takes a battering each time. When you implement and begin to respect your own boundaries, you reduce the 'ugh' feeling that comes when you've repeatedly ignored your values.

Of course, there is nothing wrong with a bit of escapism!

Only you can say where that line gets crossed for yourself. For me, I've found it helpful to leave my phone in a different room at the beginning and the end of the day when I'm with my children. These days, work and friends can wait; I got sick of the feeling that came when I was being constantly distracted. This way, my kids begin and end the day with my undivided attention, and I didn't beat myself up!

There is so much benefit to having phones. We can run our lives from the palms of our hands. They offer education, connection and increased admin efficiency. But as with so many things, there is always a flip side. And it's important to realise how they impact our self-esteem. Then we can choose to be more intentional about where we set our boundaries around phone usage and we'll notice how we feel as a result.

Disconnected connection

I hate it when people call me. I don't have the energy to chat. At the same time, I feel lonely.

Kiran

Rich, focussed connection with other people is good for our mental health. Think of the times that you've enjoyed a good conversation with someone and come away feeling encouraged, uplifted, inspired, known or supported. It's good for the mind and the soul.

Our digital world has made it so much easier to send a quick 'hope you're okay' text than pick up the phone, or arrange to meet up. Sometimes, when asked, 'How are you?' I retort with a speedy, and sometimes untrue, 'I'm fine, ta. You?' My energy is often spread so thinly that I don't have enough of it to invest in the connections and relationships I would benefit from most of all. I spend so much of my waking time communicating with people I don't know, that by the time I see my husband at the end of the day, I can manage merely grunts!

If one of your core values is that you have a few special relationships that you invest in, then that's a good core value to have! When you respect your need for quality connection, seek it out and make space for it (even when it involves some extra logistics), this will positively impact your self-esteem. Think of all the other connections you have: without the use of the internet or mobile phone, which ones would have naturally drifted by the wayside? I have gathered so many contacts in my phone over the years that I'm not even sure who many of them are. I wonder if the depth of our few meaningful relationships would increase even more, if we weren't expending energy keeping in touch superficially with those who are no longer really that present our lives.

Don't feed yourself the fast-food version of connection when you're hungry for a sit-down roast.

So why not actually pick up the phone or diarise calls if that's what you need to do? Arrange to meet someone face to face. Seek smiles and voices instead of just exchanged notes typed on a screen. Don't feed yourself the fast-food version of connection when you're hungry for a sit-down roast.

Filtered reality

I'm on the dating scene again right now. And if I go out and feel good and content, I always feel less anxious. But when I'm feeling wobbly, I just assume nobody will want to talk to me or be with me, so I kind of avoid people.

Anonymous

We are so often shown idealised characters in the media, leading us to draw unrealistic comparisons with others and to find ourselves lacking. At the touch of a screen, you can filter your face or change any element of your body to bring it into line with what we're sold as being the 'acceptable' way to look. In fact, not only are we fed filtered images of bodies, but filtered representations of lives and personalities. According to these, you should ideally be:

- Extrovert, but not too loud
- Funny, but not at all brash
- Very kind, putting everyone else first but never burning out
- Keeping all the balls in the air, but always getting eight hours sleep a night
- Working and socialising in perfect balance, and never becoming overwhelmed by either
- Warm, friendly and approachable, with never a cross or irritated word

According to this fantasy version, never a pang of PMT or a disgruntled grunt should mar your sunny disposition. Never should there be an eye rolled or a shoulder hunched. Never a word misspoken or a voice wavering. And, in the course of daily life, never a birthday forgotten, a meal cobbled together, a dirty oven or a moulding yogurt at the back of the fridge. Never a job application unsuccessful or a grade lower than an A*.

When I struggled with incredibly low self-esteem and depression, I would look around and see people seeming to live smiling, happy, fulfilled lives. I took what they displayed outwardly, and copy-and-pasted it to every other part of their lives. *If they are smiling*, I reasoned, *they must be happy.* We fill in the gaps of that which we cannot see, assuming the outer image must hold true through and through. Funnily enough, though, I kept forgetting the fact that I myself was outwardly smiling and inwardly crying, so maybe others were too.

We look outside of ourselves to find proof and confirmation that we are who we think we are. I've already mentioned how I don't like to think I might be wrong about myself; I like to think that what I believe is true. If I think I'm failing in my work, I'm going to view other people's portrayal of their work wins as proof of my failure. On the other hand, if I believe I'm worthy of friendship, I am more likely to enter relationships with a sense of confidence.

We are more vulnerable to comparison when our self-esteem has dipped. It becomes harder to argue against that critical inner voice. And with the media offering so many opportunities for us to compare ourselves to strangers, it's really helpful to begin to recognise where you are likely to fall into comparisons, so that you guard against this potentially harmful behaviour. This might mean limiting your social-media usage, or restricting how much time you spend around certain competitive friends whilst you build your resilience.

Constant feedback

I find it so hard to separate how much interaction I get on social media from strangers from those people who actually like me in real life.

Pip

These days, there is an increasing number of ways in which we can garner feedback about ourselves. Multiple-choice questionnaires tell us about our personalities. Apps provide us with constant feedback on so many areas of our lives. Algorithms inform us whether we are moving, growing, shrinking, sleeping, communicating too much or not enough. You can get data on pretty much every area and facet of your life. The thing is, these statistics rarely take into account your emotional, mental and physical capacities or how changeable you are as a human. One day you might be feeling low in energy – perhaps you are rundown or didn't sleep well – yet a notification still pops up to tell you that you haven't moved enough today.

It's like we can no longer trust what we know intuitively about ourselves. We cannot follow our hunger growls, energy levels, hormone cycles, or our personal need for slowness and rest without having this validated by some form of statistic. Sometimes I feel like I've stopped actually listening to myself, and am looking instead to digital information to tell me what I need. I can't count the number of times I've pulled up a web page and conducted an internet search on something about which my intuition is fully capable of informing me, if only I were to listen.

The digital world turns our eyes and ears away from ourselves, because it claims to be an endless fountain of knowledge. In many ways, of course it is! However, the internet cannot replace the nuance of your human thoughts and feelings, or replace the still, small, quiet voice of intuition. Instead, tiny little validations are given in the form of clicks, potentially by people you've never met. These are empty compliment calories that won't boost your self-esteem for long. Feedback is so freely given behind the shield of a screen, with fingers typing criticisms that wouldn't be said to someone's face.

The generations before us used to go through life known by fewer people. They'd maintain contact with school friends as people didn't move as far afield. These days, you may have moved from county to county, or even country to country, in search of work, love and life experiences. Yet each different postcode brings with it another group of acquaintances who haven't been privy to your past or witnessed you grow.

Today, efficiency is praised, while constant feedback serves as a signal that we are either doing well or we could do better. There is always more to aim for. I have a watch that can give me movement targets. If I hit them, it nudges them up. But when will it stop? When will it stop nudging the bar higher and higher? It has no comprehension of my personal capacity; it has no empathy for when I've been through emotional days or rough nights. It merely prompts me to make sure those stats are met, the bar reached – or it did, until I turned off the function. Media is constantly offering us ways to be more productive, to do more to a higher standard in a quicker timeframe. If your self-esteem is gained from what you do and how efficiently you do it, then you will never feel fulfilled. You will feel exhausted.

Upgrade your life

I went to my friend's new house to take a present. I got back to my house and suddenly it felt old and small. I felt fine about it before I left, but this shiny new house made mine seem dull.

Anonymous

Everything can be improved now – not just your television, from plasma screen to smart TV. Or by replacing your run-down car with a newer one. No, we are told, don't just clean your windows the old way, here are some hacks! Upgrade your brain with books, think better. Every element of life can, apparently, be better; there's a gadget, a trick, a tool, a hack for everything.

When you are told that something can be better or improved about your life or who you are, this can easily stir up a sense of dissatisfaction. It seems to point to a lack. Suddenly, something that you didn't even think was an issue turns out to need fixing, bettering or replacing. While there is nothing wrong with personal development to gain

You have the exact same worth at the beginning of any journey as at the end.

clarity or address an unhealthy habit. The problem comes when your self-esteem is pinned to that goal being met, because something else will always come along to tell you that you could be better. You'll be forever chasing a different version of yourself in the hope that you will finally be able to feel content and accept-able. Remember that you have the exact same worth at the beginning of any journey as you have at the end.

Distraction

I know when I'm feeling low because I just watch boxsets back to back until I fall asleep. It doesn't leave any space for anything else.

Anonymous

Imagine a child who is distracted from a tantrum, or a tear-fuelled moment, with a sweet or a toy. Their parent wants to save them from experiencing those difficult emotions and uses distraction to draw their attention elsewhere, to replace wails with laughter. The thing is, human emotion has purpose – even though it can feel uncomfortable, point-less or inconvenient. When you give yourself permission to feel how you feel, you let that emotion move through you, rather than halting it and hiding it. You allow it to move, to change and release. Feeling is doing; it has purpose. It might seem inconvenient or uncomfortable, but it is not pointless. When you constantly try to switch an emotion off or numb it, you just sweep that feeling under the metaphorical carpet. Things get lumpy.

Nevertheless, we often try to avoid the less pleasant emotions, such as anger, envy, grief, sadness and loneliness, by distracting ourselves with one of the myriad methods available to us. We drink, we play, we scroll, watch, clean and work. We do anything that distracts us from feeling the feelings we don't want to feel. But when we do this repeatedly, we are giving ourselves the message that those feelings aren't valid or worthy of being felt, communicated and heard. We may have learnt to do this in childhood (see chapter 2); but, with time, we can learn to add value and worth to our emotions, which will help to nurture our self-esteem.

I realised recently how I use my phone as a distraction when I'm feeling something I don't like. Stressed? Have a quick scroll until it passes, and immerse myself in someone else's world so that I can escape my own. Really, I'm not using my phone for anything other than to remove me mentally from where I am physically. I have started to treat this kind of activity as a red flag. When my screen time goes up, I take a moment to wonder what I might be trying to avoid.

When we give ourselves permission to feel emotions, they shift and change shape.

When I've worked with addicts, they often tell me that once they've stopped using, they encounter the feelings that they've been numbing themselves from. Their difficult emotions haven't gone away; their feelings have been patiently waiting for a time when that person would be able to face and experience them. When we give ourselves permission to feel emotions, they shift and change shape. I think of this process as being a bit like dumping a pile of jigsaw pieces on to the floor. Giving yourself the gift of processing emotions in a healthy way (perhaps with therapeutic support) allows you to fit the pieces together more comfortably, bringing you greater clarity and a feeling of being freed up.

Blurred boundaries

I don't sleep well and I'm sure it's because I pick up my phone whenever I wake up to see the time. Then I see an email or a message and my brain switches gear and wakes up properly.

Dana

Technology has blurred the boundaries between our work and home life. Is there even a difference anymore? The one bleeds into the other and the digital world is not going to set boundaries for us. No longer do we leave an office, clock out or press the big 'off button' on the computer. Do longer do we save our phone calls for 'off-peak' times, or keenly await a letter to drop through the letterbox from a friend. The boundaries between work and home have been flattened, mowed down by a flood of notifications, junk mail, group chats.

Technology has blurred the boundaries between work and home life.

With the immediacy of contact comes the expectation of a quick response. I wake up to messages sent to me from people all over the world. We are notified that someone has read a message and end up wondering why they haven't already replied. Shopping can be delivered on the same day that we order it online and there is very little that we have to wait for; the fast pace of life has become our new norm and we can find ourselves experiencing a wave of impatience when we have to wait for things.

So how can this impact your self-esteem? If you already feel fearful of letting people down, or of making mistakes, then these sorts of blurred boundaries and the pace of life can easily exacerbate that feeling. You may find yourself demoting your own needs for rest and separation in order to meet the needs and demands of others. My husband and I often challenge each other when we catch the other person sending a cheeky email at 11.30 p.m. We know that one of our core values is to get rest so that we can be more present the next day, be it with work or family; yet the pull of 'just this one' more email or message can feel big. The fear of being seen not to care enough, or not to show willing, can override the need for rest.

The fear of being traded in!

I remember going for my interview. It was a crazy, tense six rounds and people just got sent home at the end of each one without any explanation. I got the job but I felt on edge for at least the first year, scared to step a foot wrong because I knew people would line up to replace me.

Anonymous

I once left a job into which I'd poured a huge amount of blood, sweat and tears. I had a brief goodbye drink in the boardroom, where I was handed a card. My replacement had already been trained up and was champing at the bit to take over. I had to stop the tears from flowing. I'd given so much of myself to the role, yet when it came down to it, the fact of the matter was that I was little more than a commodity to be traded in – a minor hindrance to HR. Of course, this is often the way of modern businesses, but it's worlds away from workplaces only a generation or two ago, which tended to be smaller and more intimate. Turnovers were slower and some employees would stay in the company from the start of their career until their retirement.

So much about human interaction in this digital age feels transactional. Dating increasingly begins with a swipe right, based on looks alone. Multiple people are messaging multiple people, 'unpairing' on receiving a joke that was perhaps a little too cheesy, or because someone else comes along. Companies have higher staff turnover rates than ever, as people chase better opportunities and paycheques. The grass, it seems, is always greener.

How can this impact your self-esteem? When our self-acceptance depends on how well we feel we fit the bill, or tick the box, or on how sad people are to see us go, this world is surely a cut-throat place to be. It's so easy to take things personally when you've poured your heart and soul into a position of responsibility that you hold. It makes you human! The important thing is to recognise when you are attaching your sense of worth to a position of responsibility, because responsibilities may change but your true worth does not.

To sum up

I occasionally have this fantasy that I'll move to a remote island and live a simple, disconnected life with just a few, select loved ones. Or I imagine placing my phone calmly on the tarmac and reversing my car over it. During one of the most challenging times of my life, I used to catch myself imaging that a mysterious (non-threatening) illness would land me temporarily in hospital, where I'd get respite from the constancy of life's demands. Maybe I could believe I had value if I stepped away from everything that threatened my understanding of it.

The thing is, you cannot avoid these aspects of the world, as you will always be part of the world and the culture around you. However, it's beneficial to grow increasingly aware of the impact these distorted narratives can have on your self-esteem, and how they may sit at odds with your personal values. Awareness helps you coach yourself through these moments when you realise you're giving them power to dictate where your self-esteem lies.

JOURNAL POINTS

- What about the world around you challenges your self-esteem?
- What boundaries can you place around your use of technology to protect your self-esteem?
- Are there any relationships you'd like to invest more in? How might you take a step to do this?
- What habits do you have that might be distracting you from valid emotions?
- Would it be helpful to compartmentalise your work and home life a bit more? How can you do this?

Chapter 5

Vital vulnerability

Mantra: *I'm worthy of good relationships.*

There is nothing more vulnerable than a newborn baby. They are at the mercy of others and utterly unable to meet any of their own needs, with only gurgles and guttural noises to communicate them. They cannot control the life into which they are born, or choose which hands tend to them. The fact is that when your self-esteem is low, you may feel as vulnerable as that newborn baby. You feel at risk of attack, because you are low on the confidence that helps equalise or rationalise criticism and challenge.

There have been times in which I've felt unworthy of the love of my husband. My inner critic has been cruel and loud, affirming just how unworthy I was. I remember how my husband once commented on my haphazard tomato chopping. I was in a rush. If my self-esteem had been in a healthier place, I'd have agreed that I was at risk of severing one of my own digits! But instead, I took his comment as a criticism and felt like his small throwaway comment of 'you'd better be careful' was further proof of the fact I couldn't even chop a cherry tomato properly. He wasn't quite prepared for the sharp and tearful words he received as a retort!

Vulnerability is vital in the journey to improving your self-esteem.

I personally feel that this chapter is one of the most important parts of the book because vulnerability is abso-lutely vital in the journey to improving your self-esteem. To believe that you're worthy of good things, it's so important to feel known by others – especially by a few select people in your life. To feel known is a very powerful and validating sensation; however, one of the main things that stands in the way of our feeling known is our fear of vulnerability. So in this chapter we're going to dive deeply into exactly what vulnerability is and isn't, and we will look at how to take baby steps towards feeling more comfortable and confident in being our most authentic selves.

Vulnerability and self-worth

Cast your mind back to the big old house described in chapter 1. Remember how much there was to restore; how you had to dust and care for each tile and length of curtain? Well, now it's open to the public and people are queuing up to walk around it, and to imagine how generations before lived and loved within the house's sturdy walls. The doors are open and there are fresh dents in the soft floorboards thanks to modern footwear, and new scrapes along the walls due to jostling children. Someone has sat in an old chair, snapping the leg, and the electrics need a costly upgrade. One of the visitors has proved especially handy with a permanent marker and drawn a cartoon penis on the ancient statue. You skim the positive reviews on the house's new website, while your eyes hover tearfully over the negative ones. You feel an overwhelming desire to shut the creaking wooden doors for good. If nobody came then nobody could criticise it. But then what about the people who do enjoy it? You'd be shutting the door on all of them too.

When you let people in, it's a risk. And so often, if you feel hurt, it's tempting to shut yourself off. It's a coping mechanism, a way of protecting yourself from further pain. We are going to delve into people-pleasing in chapter 9, but for now, we are going to focus on vulnerability and attempt to take the power out of those things that find you tempted to heave shut the doors of your emotions.

How vulnerability is important for your self-esteem

Vulnerability can be transformative to your self-esteem. Often, when self-esteem is low, there is so much of yourself that you keep hidden in the hope that this will make you more acceptable to others. This creates a distance between your authentic self, the you that you know is there underneath the smiles, the pleasantries and the 'yeses'. It's the you that feels frustrated, envious, resentful, bored or irritable.

The challenge comes when you get positive feedback for the carefully curated version of yourself that you display.

You may even feel like an imposter in those relationships in which people only ever see this carefully filtered version of yourself, because, well, it was never *really* you they were seeing. You may find yourself thinking: *if they really knew me, they wouldn't think that/do that/like me/offer me that job/want to be with me.* When the real you doesn't get seen, it can be hard to believe it would ever be accepted by someone else; that you wouldn't be too much or too little or too complicated for others.

By slowly letting specific people see your authentic self and discovering that not everyone runs away with flailing arms, you can begin to believe that perhaps you are more acceptable and worthy than you initially believed. It's one of the most powerful gestures of self-care you can ever give yourself the chance of experiencing.

Me and vulnerability

For me, vulnerability is about being honest. It's the moments in which I've said, 'You know what? I'm actually not that okay', to another person. It's the moment I said I'd marry my husband. It's when I invest in friendships, letting that person know more of my inner world. It is loving my children and knowing I could lose them.

Love makes my life worth living, but it also makes me feel vulnerable because I know that nobody can put their hands on my shoulders and promise me nothing bad will happen. Vulnerability means riding a rollercoaster and trusting that the nuts and bolts are tightened regularly. It's accepting a job offer, signing a contract. It's every little situation in which I feel I've somehow invested something, be that physically or emotionally, and where I am aware I'm putting something of myself into the hands of something else.

The times in my life when I have felt most alone are also the times when I have been least vulnerable. I have been with friends and family, and I have smiled and engaged with them, yet there lay a cavernous distance between the feelings I portrayed and my feelings inside. Outside, they saw sunshine; inside, I felt heavy storm clouds. I felt seen but not known. The facade became so heavy to hold up that my arms began to shake. I started to be more open, little by little, as I worked out who I could trust with glimpses into my inner self. In time, the power was chipped away from that sense of 'if you only knew', because some people *did* know the real me. And they still cared, they still liked me, they still loved me. Not everyone understood me, but some people did, adding value to my feelings.

Even writing this book about worth is a vulnerable act. I am putting something of myself out there, with the aim of helping you to understand your worth, but this book won't just fall into the hands of people who like it: it may be disliked and criticised. So, with that risk, why do I bother to write at all? Sometimes, depending on where my self-esteem is at, when I receive the occasional criticism, my reaction can find me feeling like I want to delete everything I've ever written and just

> **When we put ourselves 'out there' in the world, we are vulnerable to criticism and opinion.**

forget it ever happened. When we put ourselves 'out there' in the world, be it embarking on a new relationship, or stepping into a new job, we are vulnerable to criticism and opinion. But think of all the things we'd have missed out on, if people hadn't taken the step to share something of themselves?

Vulnerability is . . .

Vulnerability isn't simply the act of choosing to be honest about your feelings, as I used to think it was. It's so much more wonderful and life-giving than that! Here are a few different benefits to vulnerability for you to think about.

Vulnerability is life

I've been surprised to find that the less fearful I become about being true to myself, the more I find myself embracing life itself!

Kim

By virtue of the very nature of being human, you are vulnerable. It's the state of being alive. That can seem quite a negative, foreboding statement at first glance. Because of the beliefs I've held about what vulnerability is, I've feared it in the past too. I've tried to control so many things in order to save myself from risk and vulnerability; yet, ironically, coming to terms with my vulnerability has played a key part in my starting to enjoy a less fear-based and more fulfilling life! Throughout my training as a therapist, I have learnt techniques to assist clients in exploring vulnerability and I use these tools on myself too. They do not give me immunity or build a steel wall around my heart to stop it from being broken; they just help me make sense of how to embrace aspects of vulnerability and uncertainty in my life.

Sometimes we don't feel vulnerable, we feel strong and protected. But, by the very nature of our being protected, or protecting ourselves, we are protecting something – our vulnerability!

Vulnerability is connection

I've got friends I like but sometimes I don't even think they actually know me.

Anonymous

You cannot experience rich and meaningful relationships with others without vulnerability. You would simply be a robot, exchanging codes and logic.

I remember my first relationship, which lasted for a few years. At the start we didn't fight or express our disagreements about anything. We did and said nice things that we knew the other person would enjoy. It meant that going to choose a video from the rental shop (shows my age!) would be an absolute minefield and would take more than an hour, as we tiptoed around each other's likes and dislikes, eating right into the movie time itself! Neither of us shared a true opinion, we just wanted to please each other. This was nice for a while, until it became boring and unfulfilling. In pursuit of pleasing the other person, we ignored ourselves. And in ignoring ourselves, we didn't really get to know each other!

Vulnerability is authenticity

I know those moments where I've felt understood. It's the best feeling in the world.

Zara

Vulnerability is about feeling and being seen. It's not about the facade that you feel comfortable presenting to the world, or the version of yourself that you feel is the most acceptable or likeable; it's the authentic, unfiltered you. Vulnerability is truth, your truth.

Imagine I could see into your mind and know every thought, hope, want, dislike, love, hate, hurt and dream. Imagine I could see a film of your history, every action and feeling. That intimacy would be the ultimate authenticity, the ultimate vulnerability.

Vulnerability is presence

I want to be more present with my mum as she doesn't have much time left. But it also means facing the fact that I'll miss her so much. I distract myself a lot when I'm with her, sorting and tidying, because I don't want to think about it. But then I feel sad because I wasn't actually spending time with her.

Farzad

I really want to be more present in my life and to collect my scattered thoughts, which pull me mentally in so many different directions at once. With that aim, I have days where I log out of social media, and keep my phone (my office) out of my pocket and in another room. I'm instantly more present. Yet in my presence, I'm more vulnerable. To be engaged in my life in the present moment brings me joy in many ways, but also the fear of what I risk losing: the more I love, the more love I have to lose. Nevertheless, I don't want to miss out on being present in the here and now, because I only have this one life. I must choose to risk my heart in return for the love that makes my life worth living.

When we are present, we are more vulnerable to love, to laughter, to connection.

When we are present, we are more vulnerable to love, to laughter, to connection. They are the things that make our lives worth living, yet also challenge the very core of our worth, identity and anxiety. They are two sides of the same coin: presence and vulnerability. You can't be present in the good without being vulnerable to the potential of loss.

Vulnerability is change and growth

I started therapy to finally talk about my uncle. It has been hard opening up, but each week I feel like more of the weight that I've carried is lifted, making space for light.

Anonymous

You cannot change and grow without acknowledging areas of lack and weakness. You cannot clean that big old house without first opening the door to see what needs to be cleaned inside. As you acknowledge your vulnerability while choosing to step into new situations and relationships, you cannot remain unchanged in some way – big or small. You are never the same, from one day to the next. You are not the same as you were yesterday, because time has passed and you have been changed and shaped by the experiences you've had. As you live more authentically, you change and grow to become more ... you.

Vulnerability is risky

It became a running joke that I was a four-date wonder. I'd start liking someone and then I'd cut it off because I was scared of getting hurt.

Anonymous

Whilst there is, of course, risk in showing vulnerability, there is also risk in avoiding it. There is the very real risk that you will not live your fullest life, that your worth will not be enjoyed by others, and that you will not fulfil your purpose because you are held back by fear. Life is about risk, but to risk shutting down your emotional life from fear that the costs will be too high is to walk away from so much potential for joy, laughter, connection and purpose.

As I mentioned previously, I broke up with my boyfriend (now husband) many times when we were dating. The risk of loving felt high as I'd been hurt previously. In the end, I took the risk – and I'm glad I did!

Vulnerability is sometimes a choice

I had to be honest with my boss about my mental health because I was making so many excuses for why I was turning down all the client events last Christmas. He hooked me up with a counselling service, I'm so glad I said.

Kim

Life is made up of a series of choices. We make conscious choices, like whether we accept a new job or not, or what we eat for breakfast. Sometimes, however, the choices we make aren't conscious; they have become our automatic ways of being and living. An example of this would be how you respond to someone making fun of you – they are those knee-jerk reactions that bubble up and spill over.

There are also many vulnerabilities that, no matter how hard you may try, you cannot protect yourself against. You can make decisions that keep your body as healthy as possible. You can choose to eat a balanced diet, or to put your running shoes on. Sure, you can decrease your chances of certain illnesses, but you cannot immunise yourself against everything. You can increase your personal safety – you can drive sensibly, look both ways when you cross the road, lock your doors and board up the window – but you cannot completely protect yourself from the whipping winds of life's metaphorical hurricanes.

We are all vulnerable, but being emotionally vulnerable in this way is a choice. Showing and sharing your inner self to someone is a choice that will have an impact on you, your future, your support network and your self-esteem.

What vulnerability isn't

Vulnerability isn't manipulation

My brother literally used to use our childhood experience as a way to get girls to feel sorry for him. It used to make me angry because it was private to me. It worked, though!

Anonymous

In its true form, vulnerability isn't a tactic to get people to like you. Being vulnerable with the right people is an amazing way of nurturing self-esteem. However, when we are open about something with an aim of getting someone to like or feel sorry for us, this lacks authenticity; therefore any connection we gain is of the artificial type, rather than the kind that comes from having your authentic self affirmed.

If I speak about my experience of post-natal depression in order to provoke sympathy rather than connection, this cannot truly boost my self-esteem because it isn't authentically driven. If I speak of experience in order to help others out of compassion, or a need to feel supported, the sense of purpose is more affirming.

Vulnerability isn't weakness

The day I told my friend I didn't like the way she spoke to me, after eight years, was the day I had a whole new respect for myself. I felt scared and proud.

Francine

Vulnerability doesn't immediately make people think of strength. However, choosing to be emotionally vulnerable in the right context requires bravery, consideration and strength.

When I've chosen to be emotionally honest, it sure hasn't felt like a weak thing to do. I've stood up on trembling legs, with a wavering voice. My defence mechanisms have threatened to pull up the drawbridge faster than I can say, 'I'd love to speak to you about something . . .' Vulnerability, for me, has been to say 'no' when my people-pleasing drive wills me to say 'yes'. It is getting behind a steering wheel, picking up the phone, trying for a baby. It's in the difficult conversations that I'd much rather put off. It's ending contracts and signing for new ones. All of those things are statements of value. These are the self-esteem boosting decisions that say: 'My voice, my needs, feelings, opinions and experiences are just as valid as anyone else's.' If vulnerability were a weakness, it would be easier. Vulnerability requires a special form of emotional strength.

When being strong isn't helpful for your self-esteem

> *We had a whole year where it felt like everything went wrong. I was so strong, everyone said so. And then when things calmed down, I broke.*

> Anonymous

Strength is often hailed as a desirable characteristic, something to be applauded. But sometimes strength can be a coping mechanism. Many of my coaching and therapy clients say things along the lines of, 'When things were tough, I was so strong and I coped so well, but now I'm a mess . . .' Often we are strong because we have to be. But to be strong in this way, we might have to overlook emotion. Think of the marathon runner who finishes the race – only to realise that his leg hurts badly. He has a stress fracture, but his adrenalin enabled him to run through the pain. Just because he didn't feel pain as he ran doesn't mean his leg wasn't broken. His mind and body just chose not to feel the pain in order to get him through the race. Sometimes you have to ignore emotions in order to keep on keeping on, but this survival technique can so easily become a way of life.

A survival mechanism is intended to last for short periods of time until we feel safe enough to process our feelings, but it can sometimes run away with us and become a habit. When I lost my sister, my way of surviving was to tuck my grief away so that I could be strong for those around me. I ignored my feelings, which in turn, devalued them. This became my blueprint default mechanism for dealing with life's challenges. Vulnerability became a scary thing to me. What would happen if I were to be honest about how I felt? I might never be the same again! Little did I know how true that would be . . . I would never be the same again. In a good way.

Vulnerability continues to change my life – and I don't want to go back behind my walls. It was safer there in some respects, but it was lonely when the only person who truly knew me was me. There are things in my life today that find me unintentionally lowering my drawbridge and revealing more of my authentic feelings. I find that hormones, stress and tiredness lessen the energy I have to power through the day, but perhaps what is being revealed is simply what has been there all along.

Signs that vulnerability is a challenge

Here are some examples to help you gain clarity on how vulnerability can be a challenge. It's okay to identify with more than a couple of them; I personally relate to every single one!

- You prefer to be the one asking others questions than being the one asked.
- If you're asked a question you don't want to answer, you may overshare, to alleviate awkwardness, and later regret it.
- You'd rather stick to superficial topics such as work, holiday plans or the weather.
- If you are offended, you find it easier to brush it under the carpet than discuss it.
- You don't like being the centre of attention unless you are feeling confident.
- You feel like you're a different version of yourself around different people.
- You find it difficult to choose who to be open with.
- Not many of your friends really know how you feel.
- You prefer to help and support others than be helped or supported.

- You find yourself feeling, 'But if they really knew me, they'd reject me . . .'
- You find it hard to receive kind words, compliments and criticisms.
- You feel like an imposter in areas where you are doing well.
- You find yourself sabotaging relationships as you begin to feel close to someone.

The more you recognise what your fear of vulnerability is protecting you from, the more likely you are to notice the opportunities that invite you to step out into authenticity.

You worry about being judged

I realised I'd found it so hard to be open with people because my mum always just used to say, 'Look on the bright side, look for the silver lining.'

Anonymous

My experience as a therapist has taught me that we are all vulnerable. We all have rough edges and dark corners. All of us. It has been incredibly freeing to come to

We are all vulnerable.

terms with the fact that whilst the nature of my own messiness might be unique, I am certainly not unique in having mess behind the scenes – and in front of the scenes too! The more I've accepted this fact, the more comfortable I have felt about verbalising it.

If you tend to judge yourself harshly, it's common to assume that others judge you harshly too. Some people may do that, but most will not; and even if they do, that often says more about their level of insight and understanding than it does about you.

When you've been hurt

I used to have this whole rule that if someone hurt me once, I'd cut them out completely.

Anonymous

When you've been hurt or let down, it can be scary even to think about risking being vulnerable with someone again. It's helpful to be wary of black-and-white attitudes and to soften them. Turn 'see, nobody understands me' into 'he didn't understand me, but someone else might'. As we know, it's often easy to take someone's behaviour as a reflection or a statement of who you are, when it's actually just an indication of where they're at and their ability to support you. If your vulnerability has been abused in some way, or you find it very hard to open up after being hurt, therapy can help you grow in confidence again. (See Helpful Contacts, page 265.)

You don't have to tell everyone everything

When I started talking about my addiction, it felt like I had to be open with everyone. Then my sober friend told me that it's helpful to have some 'top-liners' to dish out according to who I was talking to and how much detail I felt safe going into. It made me feel safer.

Anonymous

Not everyone needs to know everything. Whichever friend, family member or therapist gets to glimpse beyond your 'I'm okay', remember that it is an honour to know your story and see behind the scenes. Sometimes vulnerability is a case of lowering your guard so that you can connect with people and experiences more authentically. Yet occasionally you need to put up the guard and establish healthy boundaries that allow you to develop confidence over time! You don't need to rip off the plaster when it comes to sharing your wounds and addressing your self-esteem; otherwise you may feel overwhelmed and be tempted to shut yourself off. You have every right to say no to any probing questions that you don't feel comfortable answering.

Not everyone needs to know everything.

Thanks to the good old people-pleasing drive, I've sometimes found myself saying more about myself than I've been comfortable with. I used to have a friend who would ask direct questions that I would answer because I didn't want to make things awkward between us. She would then use the sensitive information I'd shared with her as material for gossip, just as she did with other people's honest disclosures.

I tried to set boundaries so that the friendship could continue in a way that felt healthy and respectful, but sadly she didn't feel able to respect these and the relationship had to come to an end.

The post-vulnerability regret

I told my doctor about how I'd been feeling and left the appointment so embarrassed. I couldn't believe I'd said it all out loud. I had to keep reassuring myself that she'd probably heard it all before.

Anonymous

Have you ever had that dream where you realise you're naked in public? Vulnerability can feel a bit like that. You feel exposed. You want to throw your armour back on and pretend it never happened. You might feel this way because you shared something about yourself with an individual who wasn't able to respond in the way you needed them to, perhaps due to their own prejudices or emotional capacity.

When someone responds in a way that feels hurtful or dismissive of you, it's tempting to use that as proof that you should hike up the drawbridge and pledge never to utter those words, assert that boundary, or speak about that topic again! But I'd ask you to guard against taking another person's response and turning it into a statement that undermines your feelings and experiences. When you lift the drawbridge to protect yourself from being misunderstood, you deny yourself the opportunity to feel understood too.

Sometimes I experience that wave of regret even though

I've felt understood and validated. I'm so used to feeling shame about particular parts of myself that once something's out in the open, I want to inject the other person with a magic serum to wipe their memory of it. My shame or sense of guilt sweeps in with fear of judgement or worry that my vulnerability will be abused and my words used as gossip fodder. In time, as I've strengthened the muscle of vulnerability, this sense of regret has become less pertinent. It's more of a passing wave than an enveloping tide.

Who should you be open with?

I had a coaching session with Anna and she encouraged me to speak honestly with a particular friend. She was so kind even though she hadn't been through the same thing; it gave me confidence to speak to someone else.

Anonymous

When it comes to being open with others, I encourage clients to begin with a support network of two. Choose those people who have been historically kind and supportive to you. You might well choose a therapist. We professionals are bound by codes of ethics to offer complete confidentiality, so therapy can be a great way to develop confidence in talking about the things you find tough.

Imagine vulnerability as a muscle. As you use it, you strengthen it.

Imagine vulnerability as a muscle. As you use it, you strengthen it. The best way to strengthen a muscle is to do so over time, in increments, as you develop confidence. Slow and steady growth is the most sustainable. Bit by bit and little by little. Harsh, quick muscle building is more likely to leave you sore or in pain. In the same way, take risks around vulnerability that nudge you gently outside your comfort zone.

Notice the opportunities that arise where you could step a toe outside that zone. Perhaps you're with a friend who you could ask to help you with something. Maybe it's the chance to say 'no' where before you may have automatically said 'yes'. Maybe it's an honest reply to a friend who asks how you are, instead of your usual, 'Fine, ta – and you?' Those are opportunities to experiment with vulnerability and test the water. If your friend responds kindly, perhaps next time you might feel able to take a step, or ask more confidently to have your needs met.

To be known is to be loved

When I started to be kinder to myself, it became easier to accept kindness from my mates.

Vee

I can't say I love a country I've not been to. I love the idea of it, perhaps – the photos I've seen of it and what other people have shared about their holidays there. But if I've only visited one small town, can I say I love the country? Not

The more you are known, the more potential you have to be loved.

really, I haven't experienced the whole thing, but I sure can say I love what I've seen.

It's the same with you. We can only truly love what we know; and the more you are known, the more potential you have to be loved. As you become more authentic in your relationships, the more fulfilling they can become. When you have a good, honest conversation with someone, you 'see' and know more of one another. And where there is openness and honesty, there is less suspicion. Your mind constantly fills in the gap that sits between what you know about someone, and what you don't, with assumptions. The more you really know someone, the less you relate to the version of them you have in your head. In the first week of dating my husband, he told me he loved me. Then he kept changing his mind. I didn't mind because I knew he didn't really know me. How could he love what he didn't know? We laugh about this now. But to really feel loved, we need to feel known.

You will never feel truly acceptable if you do not accept yourself.

Can anyone really know all of you? And can you ever feel truly lovable if not?

I think so. I think it's possible to feel loved and known, even if someone doesn't know every little thought and experience you've ever had. I think we just have to accept that in order to feel acceptable, we need to find a way to accept ourselves. You have worth regardless of the secrets you keep.

Ultimately, you will never feel truly acceptable if you do not accept yourself. You will never feel worthy of compassion if you cannot find compassion for yourself. Forgiveness, patience, kindness, support – these are all things you need to offer yourself so that you feel worthy of accepting them from others. In order to take the risk of being known, we need to address the shame and guilt that find us keeping some of our needs and feelings hidden.

To sum up

Vulnerability is one of the most important tools for strengthening self-esteem. It enables you to be loved and validated. You deserve to feel understood, respected and supported. Vulnerability is also a vital weapon in the fight against two of the main enemies of healthy self-esteem: shame and guilt. And that's what we're going to be looking at in the next chapter.

JOURNAL POINTS

- What does vulnerability mean to you?
- When has vulnerability been a positive turning point for you in some way?
- What stops you from being open with people about how you feel?
- When have you felt known and supported by others?
- Which two people in your life might you like to be more honest with?

Chapter 6

The enemies of self-esteem

Mantra: *Guilt is there to prompt me, not to shame me.*

Guilt and shame are not the same thing, even though the words are occasionally used interchangeably. Sometimes you may not realise that what you are experiencing is guilt or shame, because these emotions can come out through different behaviours and feelings. You might think that someone 'should' only feel guilt when they have done something wrong, or feel shame if they are a bad person. But truthfully, we can feel guilty and ashamed regardless of how we've behaved.

Guilt and shame push down self-esteem and make us feel unworthy of the good things in life. This is because when you feel unworthy, you're more likely to experience guilt and shame. It becomes a bit of a downward spiral. Recognising how guilt and shame impact your life means that you can address them. So, in the next few pages, we're going to explore these challenging feelings. It might feel like getting on a mini rollercoaster, but bear with me ...

My hope is that by the end of this chapter, you'll step off the rollercoaster, with more compassion for yourself and less shame and guilt.

Guilt and self-esteem

I literally feel guilty every day about something or another. And then, because I feel bad, I overthink about what I should have done differently.

Freya

Guilt is a very familiar feeling for so many of us. I have felt a lot of guilt in my life – about things I've done wrong when I didn't really know better, and things I've taken responsibility for that were not mine to take ownership of. I've felt guilty for saying no; guilty for asking for help; guilty for struggling; guilty for not being honest. I've felt guilty for not calling someone, and for calling someone; for speaking out, for not speaking out. Guilty for sharing, for not sharing; for wanting more; for forgetting someone's birthday; having needs and feeling hurt, annoyed or resentful. Lots of guilt!

Guilt tends to be focussed on a specific act or circumstance. For example, I felt tremendous guilt at struggling to bond with my second child due to his reflux; it was the gap between what I expected I *should* feel and what I actually felt that caused the sense of guilt for me. Because I felt guilty, I didn't feel deserving of being his mum. And because I struggled to connect with him, I concluded that I didn't deserve the experience of motherhood, which so many desperately want. This sense of guilt just reinforced my low self-esteem. My inner critic worked to affirm how I felt, telling me that I wasn't good enough for my kids or my husband. I was a sad failure who didn't deserve the support available to me. Didn't everyone know how bad a person I was? My friends wouldn't be my friends if they had insight into the dark thoughts inside my mind, surely?

In most of my therapeutic work, we discuss guilt. Whether my clients feel they've failed to meet the expectations of others, or are carrying a sense of responsibility for something they haven't actually done wrong, guilt features in all therapeutic journeys. Guilt has a huge impact on mental health, which is why it is so important to address it. Often we give great weight to these sorts of feelings, believing that if we feel guilty, we must *be* guilty. Let me tell you this:

- Feelings aren't facts.
- You might feel guilty – but it doesn't mean you are.
- If you're finding ways to punish yourself to bring some sort of equilibrium, this will negatively impact your self-esteem.

You do not deserve to be punished for things you haven't done.

You do not deserve to be punished for things you haven't done. And as for the things you have done wrong? What about those? Well, even prisoners are acquitted after they've served their time. There comes a point when you have to let yourself off the hook.

Guilt is not intended to act like a big black rock for you to carry around for your whole life. When guilt sits in your stomach, you feel like you've done something wrong. Maybe you have, maybe you haven't. But regardless of whether you've committed a crime, or just feel guilty because your moods have been low and people around you haven't had the best of you for a few days, that sensation needs addressing.

When you don't address guilt, you may try to ease it through punishing behaviour. This is based on the idea that yin needs yang, and a debt needs paying – otherwise it affects your credit rating. It's like doing jail time for a crime. To ease the guilt, you offset it with punishment. Perhaps you sabotage a good opportunity or a relationship you don't feel you deserve. Perhaps your critical internal dialogue gets a bit crueller, or you try to be extra pleasing or giving as a way of righting a wrong – like some kind of personal community service.

The guilt debt

If I'm feeling happy in myself, I notice that I don't take things quite so personally.

Sash

If your self-esteem is low, you may be letting guilt overly influence who you understand yourself to be. For me, unaddressed guilt would sit like a growling animal in my stomach. And no amount of good deeds, self-deprecation, self-destructiveness, self-sabotage or people-pleasing could feed the hungry beast enough for him to leave me be. If we equate guilt with owing a debt, the lower our self-esteem, the more harshly we are likely to judge the cost of that debt.

When I've unintentionally upset a friend, for example, low self-esteem will find me making black-and-white statements about myself, such as: *I'm a bad friend, I hurt people. I don't deserve good friends.* I'll be more likely to over-apologise and feel driven to over-please. Say I was to unintentionally upset a friend when my self-esteem was in a better place: then, I'd find it easier to coach myself through the feeling, knowing that I can be a good friend – because the evidence is there! I'd view the situation more rationally, finding it easier to approach the friend for a conversation. The sense of guilt wouldn't be a statement of who I am, but an indicator of what has gone wrong and what might merit an apology.

Challenging guilt

Too often guilt goes unchallenged. In fact, challenging the feeling of guilt has been life-changing for me. Now, I want to share an insight that changed the entire way I experience guilt: guilt is there to prompt us, not to shame us. It serves as a flag that there's a feeling that needs to be addressed by taking action.

I created a technique to help with how I responded to guilt. I still use it often and recommend it to my clients. I use the acronym ACT to remind myself that guilt is there to prompt me and not serve as a constant reminder of how undeserving I am of the good things in my life.

A = address the guilt

Imagine the guilt as a sooty lump of coal. Now take that lump of coal in your hand and ask yourself exactly what it is. What is the belief? What have you done or not done, felt or not felt, thought or not thought? Let's think of an example: I feel guilty for lying about not being available to celebrate a friend's birthday when I actually was.

C = compassion

Now, you'll have to trust me on this next point, because it can feel so hard to believe. Whatever you feel guilty about, you are deserving of compassion. Whether you have stolen a penny sweet, evaded responsibility, lied, or hurt a friend – there will be a reason that you deserve compassion somehow. Without compassion for yourself, you cannot properly let guilt do what it needs to do – and that is to prompt you, not shame you. Think of how you would speak to a friend; how would you advise them if they felt guilty about missing a birthday celebration? What was the bigger picture, the history that may have led to them feeling or acting a certain way?

Injecting compassion isn't about removing responsibility where it is due. It's not about excusing or forgetting. It's about introducing the valuable perspective that is often lost when our self-esteem is low. It's about remembering that you are human, you are imperfect, you have histories and traumas that get triggered whether you are aware of it or not. Imagine speaking to a murderer on death row, who has spent a life sentence in a cell to account for the lives he viciously claimed. Yet if you heard his story, his history, his shame, his remorse, you'd most likely find compassion. Compassion doesn't right a wrong. It acknowledges the inherent worth we all have.

You are a complex mess of humanity, of light and dark. You deserve to take responsibility for your wrongs, within reason, and also to let go of responsibility where it's not due and to experience compassion along the way. You can hold yourself responsible – with compassion. Compassion is the light to the darkness of guilt, bringing clarity and movement to what would otherwise keep you stuck and feeling undeserving of the good things in your life.

I must note briefly here that there are some people who aren't able to exhibit remorse or guilt. In these instances, there may be a concealing or denial of guilt, a constant blaming on another person to absolve themselves of responsibility. The lack of any true sense of guilt or empathy, where due, tends to be a pathological symptom. These characteristics may require further psychological insight or assessment.

So, back to my example of lying about being available for my friend's birthday celebration. How might I bring in compassion? Say I had only had three and a half hours' sleep the night before. I was hormonal, which always has an impact on my ability to think rationally and wait a beat before I respond. Even though I'm a people-pleaser in recovery, I generally try to be honest about my availability and my reasons for not being able to do something. I deserve compassion. I'm low in resources and my fib came from a place of not wanting to offend her. This is not to say it was right to lie, that I did the right thing. Lying conflicted with my own core values and I was responsible for choosing to lie. I can give myself compassion whilst also taking responsibility.

T = tweak something

If guilt is there to prompt you into action, how might you respond to it? Perhaps you've identified that the guilt you've been carrying isn't actually your respon-

Guilt is there to prompt you into action.

sibility. How might you relinquish a sense of responsibility, or hand it back to someone else in some way, whether through changing the way you think about it, or through a conversation with that individual or a therapist? Once you've decided to let go of the guilt, put that black, sooty bit of coal down on the floor. It's not yours anymore.

For me, the guilt about lying to my friend is there to prompt me to act. Maybe I drop her a text to say, 'I'm so sorry I didn't come tonight. I'm feeling absolutely floored by a few rough nights with the kids and am heading to bed early – but I didn't want to tell you and upset you. Can we get something in the diary so we can celebrate and have a proper catch-up? I'm sad to miss out and hope you have a fab time.'

A sense of guilt may be prompting you to find new tools or the clarity to deal with the situation differently, should it arise again. In fact, even when you've been through the ACT process, that same sense of guilt may pop back up! Remind yourself that you have already addressed it. You've taken action, it's not needed anymore. Often carrying guilt has become a habit that has helped prove your sense of failure or of not being enough. Guilt might have been the lens through which you viewed the world and whether you were worthy of good things. You've believed you aren't worthy of being forgiven, or of forgiving yourself (which, after all, is an act of kindness). Happily, habits can be changed and although guilt has purpose, you don't need to check yourself into death row over a small act.

Imagine if a friend upset you and you knew their motivations weren't intentionally cruel. They've made a heartfelt apology, yet you keep making them pay, over and over. You ask them for favours at every possible opportunity and use it as an excuse to be irritable and snappy with them. Just when they think you've forgiven them and begin to feel secure in your friendship, you remind them of their slip-up. Would that be fair? Would you do this to someone else? No! Then why do you do it to yourself? Blame without compassion will keep you stuck.

Let yourself off the hook and move on.

I hope that has helped you reframe guilt a little. Next time you feel that familiar wave wash over you, grab that lump of coal in your hand, journey through ACT, and then set it down. When guilt tries to lurch back into your stomach about that same issue, place it down. It has served its purpose. You've done your time. You deserve to let yourself off the hook and move on.

Sometimes someone will hold on to a wrong you've committed long after you've apologised. Their anger and lack of forgiveness is their own emotional response; you cannot be held responsible for how they react to your apology, only they can. If you've mindfully addressed your wrongdoing, it's good to respect that the other person may need time to process their feelings, and that your relationship may perhaps change shape. You can face the consequences of your actions whilst also allowing yourself to move forwards. When you let other people's emotional journeys dictate how long you should feel guilt for, the process becomes stuck and impacts your self-esteem.

Shame and self-esteem

I have this constant feeling that I'm a bad person and that I don't deserve my boyfriend.

Anonymous

Shame is a sense of failing to live up to an ideal. It perpetuates a deep and sometimes consistent feeling of not being good enough or worthy of good things, experiences and relationships. It can be the background noise to which we live, and could have been there for most of our life in some way or another. Shame can begin in childhood, especially if you believed you were not good enough for your caregivers, or their standards seemed unattainable. Shame can make you feel inherently flawed, like you need to hide a part of yourself or constantly compensate for it.

Shame has driven me to strive ever harder for academic success and to go out of my way for others at the cost of my own resources. All in the hope that I might finally feel like I've earned the status of 'good enough' to be deserving of the good things in my life.

Is embarrassment the same as shame?

I'll mention embarrassment so that we can separate it from shame. We all know that feeling. Embarrassment is usually triggered by a specific event or circumstance, often in full view of others. It's like a mild and temporary form of shame. However, it may add to an existing feeling of shame around the issue in hand.

I knocked out my front teeth when I was ten. I tumbled over the handlebars of my bike whilst going uphill. (I know, I know, don't ask!) One front tooth fell out, clean onto the ground. The other tooth hung on for dear life. We sped to the nearest hospital where a visiting dentist slotted them back into my jaw and stuck them in place with dental cement, in the hope they'd bed back in. They did, but at such jaunty angles that it meant you could see flashes of greying white even when I had my lips closed. I hated my front teeth, and it was hard to find an orthodontist who felt confident enough to approach them with moulds and braces.

Kids can be so cruel, and I have such memories of the embarrassment I felt when I was called names like 'rabbit' and ridiculed. My face would turn a shade of beetroot, I could feel the warmth rise from my toes to my hair and I wanted to disappear. Had I not already felt a sense of shame about who I was, this feeling of embarrassment may have evaporated once the moment had passed and when I was with those who made me feel safe and secure in who I was. But even now, with some of my upper jaw rebuilt by synthetic bone and after several sets of orthodontic braces, screws, implants and veneers, I still sometimes catch myself trying to smile in a way that hides my teeth.

So, shame and embarrassment do cross over a bit, but they are not the same. Embarrassment is temporary and changes with our level of self-esteem. What we assume others think about us has a big impact on our level of embarrassment. If I assume everyone is laughing at me secretly, I will have more fear of silent ridicule should I discover my skirt is tucked into my pants. Afterwards, I may even find myself cringing every time the memory of it springs to mind. But if my self-esteem is healthy, I may laugh awkwardly, untuck it and carry on with my day!

How does shame feel?

Can you describe how shame feels in your body? I find it comes over me very suddenly when I feel like I am being challenged in a personal, uncomfortable way. The feeling might rise up if someone shouts at me, or tells me that I've done wrong, or hurt them. It may be that I open a challenging or critical email. In an instant, it feels like the wind has been slapped out of my chest and replaced with hot coals. My heart beats faster, I feel shaky and sick. I can think of nothing else around me, other than the situation. It kicks my body into the fight-or-flight stress response and I immediately scrabble for a way out. When I feel shame, I feel worthless. And my behaviour very quickly becomes self-destructive and self-punishing. My inner critic grabs a microphone, turns the volume to max and screams worthlessness into the corners of my mind.

Feeling shame taps into a sense of unworthiness deep down inside, as if it has drawn this out and exposed it for all to see. I feel naked and attacked. If I feel shame, I might try to justify myself, or I could even be tempted to pin the blame on another person in an argument. I might twist an argument round, using it to attack whoever seems to be holding me to account, making them the bad person instead and reclaiming a sense of power. When we feel shame, a very basic drive to protect ourselves is activated, sending rationality flying out of the window. You may find yourself doing, saying or acting in ways that don't really fit with who you believe and know yourself to be.

Shame may find you feeling like you want to remove the sense of responsibility because it is so emotionally and physically uncomfortable. It can be hard to find compassion and empathy for yourself. Now, it is helpful here not to try to defend yourself against shame, but to develop ways to help move you out of that stress response feeling, first by identifying what this is. When we feel shame, our behaviours and responses are motivated by fear and stress. Our aim is to get to a place of physical and emotional safety as quickly as possible. We need to alleviate the uncomfortable things we are experiencing and remove risk of further pain. There are three stress responses:

Fight: this is an angry, active, fighting response. You may feel driven to destroy somehow the thing that is causing you shame. The energy feels like a volcano erupting, and you want to (and take moves to) somehow disempower the thing causing you pain.

Flight: you run from the trigger of your shame. You try to avoid or escape it, perhaps physically taking yourself away from the situation.

Freeze: you submit to the threat. You don't fight it or run away from it, you let it happen. This is a last resort that kicks in when the source of shame feels too overpowering, and neither fighting nor fleeing seems to be an option.

Instead of giving in to these impulses, try breathing in for a count of four and then breathing out for a count of six. Do this ten times. This type of breathing will help to calm your sympathetic nervous system stress response, and enable you to regain clarity. It signals to your body that you are safe, so that all of the physical feelings (increased heart rate, sweating, nausea, etc.) can recede. When your breathing calms, you can begin to access a more rational, grounded type of thinking. The rational part of your brain allows you to view situations more subjectively and clearly. It's like stepping out of the cloud of emotion, stress and fear, and being able to view the situation from an outside perspective.

The next step is to understand what has caused the feeling of shame. Check in with yourself and ask yourself some questions in the way you would ask a friend:

- What happened?
- What are you feeling?
- Are you okay?
- In the moment shame hit, what were you believing about yourself?

- What statements were going through your mind?
- Where did this message originate?
- What are the facts?
- What do you need?
- Do you feel guilty about something? (Use the ACT tool if so.)

Here's an example of an experience of mine:

- What happened?
  A man called me 'stupid woman' when I hit a kerb parking.

- What are you feeling?
  Angry and upset.

- Are you okay?
  I feel sick! It's really impacted me.

- In the moment shame hit, what were you believing about yourself?
  That he was right.

- What statements were going through your mind?
  'I'm stupid. I'm a failure. I'm worthless.'

- Where did this message originate?
  Someone important to me would call me stupid and it would make me feel like I would never be good enough for them.

- What are the facts?
  That I might do silly things, or make mistakes, but I also get things right and do good things too.

- What do you need?
  To remind myself that I am not stupid; that this was just the man's judgement.

- Do you feel guilty about something? Use the ACT tool if so.
  I don't feel guilty in this instance.

Going through this process gives you an opportunity to regulate your emotions and move through the feeling rather than remain stuck in it, which is a very painful and unhelpful place to be. You might be able to recognise feelings or triggers that are familiar to you; and perhaps you could benefit from more professional guidance or therapeutic insight to tackle them.

Why do we feel shame?

We are all subject to lots of different rules and expectations that tell us whether something is right or wrong. My understanding of how I believe it's right to feel and behave has been influenced by my upbringing, my experience of attending church from a young age, my culture and the way my family interpret and respond to rules, laws and ethics. I have my own list of 'shoulds and shouldn'ts' – some that need to be challenged, some that are set in stone and some that change like the weather. They all work together to determine my likelihood to feel shame and form my own unique shame barometer.

Let's look in a little more detail at some aspects of our lives that influence how we experience shame.

The cultures you are exposed to

> *I grew up in a country that isn't as accepting of homosexuality as where I live now. My brother came out as gay in the nineties and my whole family got treated like there was something wrong with us and I was bullied at school.*
>
> Anonymous

Perhaps you were brought up in a collectivist culture, where the emphasis is on family and community? Some cultures stigmatise particular groups or individual characteristics, viewing certain topics, such as sexuality, as taboo. In response, certain members of the community can understandably believe that their authentic self is unacceptable. There are also religions which place great emphasis on being 'good', using shame to condition behaviour. If an element of your character or experience feels somehow taboo or unacceptable, your feelings of shame may be increased. In other instances, where there is tight social cohesion, the perceived wrongs of individuals can impact the wider community. For example, if someone has an affair, the parents and wider family may be judged too, prompting wider shame.

Because you have been shamed by someone else

I remember being little, I used to feel scared sometimes and would wet myself. My whole family would laugh at me, calling me 'pissy pants'. It just made me more fearful of it happening. I was a joke to them.

Anonymous

Shaming behaviour is sometimes used as a way to control or punish. At its most obvious, in the past people were paraded through the streets, attacked publicly, or had their basic rights removed. Today, shaming behaviour happens frequently online, but it can manifest itself in other more insidious ways. Shaming targets what someone is, not what they have done. Instead of saying 'that wasn't a kind thing to do', shaming is saying 'you are bad and unworthy'.

Shaming behaviour is sometimes used as a way to control or punish.

Causing someone to feel shame can be deeply impacting and can be done in both very obvious ways and very nuanced ways throughout our lives. It can make us feel ashamed of who we are. Examples include being constantly compared to a sibling, or being ridiculed about a characteristic or personality trait. Shame promotes the feeling of our not being good enough.

Because you have taken responsibility where you
didn't need to

> *I was bullied at work by a manager. If I spoke to her about it, she*
> *said she was just pushing me because she saw potential in me. And*
> *that if I wanted to leave, I should, as there would be twenty people*
> *lining up for my job. So I put up with it for years.*

Anonymous

You may be experiencing shame because you have repeatedly taken responsibility for something that has been done to
you, or because of the way in which you have been treated
by someone else or the system. To justify certain behaviours,
a person who has shamed someone might place blame on
their victim: 'I'm treating you like this because you're a bad
child' or 'you asked for this'. They want to avoid accepting
the responsibility that belongs to them, so that they don't
have to feel guilty. But nobody deserves to hold themselves
responsible for the decisions made by someone else.

Perhaps you have had to ignore your own hurt so that an
important relationship could continue. An example of this
is when a child has no other choice but to let their caregiver
continue bullying or mistreating them. Perhaps they cannot
risk putting up a fight and then being treated worse or punished even further.

If you have been in a relationship in which there is an
element of gaslighting, this increases feelings of shame.
Gaslighting is a form of manipulation where you are caused
to question your own sanity. Some examples of gaslighting
statements are: *you're being hysterical*; *you're talking rubbish*; *you're*

mad, I never said that; you're being oversensitive. Gaslighting behaviours are used in order for the perpetrator to gain power and make their victim question their own reality and the validity of their feelings, thoughts and experiences. Imagine a gaslit lantern: gaslighting is like turning up the gas and then shouting at the flames for getting larger!

Because your standards are very high

Whenever anything bad happens I assume it must be my fault.

Toni

If your standards are high and your self-forgiveness is low, you are more likely to experience shame. Like many of us, I have a habit of allowing myself only the slimmest margin for error. I live to the wire, leaving the house without a moment to spare, cramming my diary in a way that forces me to rush around from one thing to another. I juggle too many balls and wear too many hats, but then criticise myself as soon as one tumbles or slips. If you also set yourself up to fall and fail, then your inner critic is going to be getting a lot more airtime.

When your self-esteem is low, you are more likely to blame yourself for matters that may well be due to the circumstances. You take responsibility quickly – and often where it might not even be your responsibility to accept. When things go awry, your mind searches for explanations. You may blame someone else, a situation or circumstance, the bad weather or a delayed train. But when you consistently blame yourself, and ignore any relevant external factors, you can end up taking too much responsibility – leading to guilt, self-criticism and shame, all of which damage self-esteem.

For example, I had periods of blaming myself for my post-natal depression. At those times, I'd feel deep guilt and shame. I'd blame myself for not meeting my ideal as a grateful, happy and doting second-time mum who 'should' be enjoying the wonderful bubble of newborn life. I blamed myself for not being able to replicate the images I'd seen so many times as I scrolled blurry-eyed through social-media feeds. But when I took into account environmental factors such as chronic sleep deprivation, my baby's relentless screaming, or the fact we were trying to move house at the same time, it introduced a more balanced view. It enabled me to inject some compassion into the situation, just as I would want to do if a friend were beating herself up and feeling ashamed for the same thing.

Because you shame yourself for certain feelings

Every time I feel jealous that someone else has a baby and I don't, I get angry with myself. I should be happy for them. I'm trying to remember that envy is a normal human emotion and it's understandable.

Anonymous

It can be so tempting to grab the gratitude stick and beat yourself over the head with it. Gratitude can be an incredible tool for drawing our attention away from focussing on what is hard, sad and worrying so that we can see the bigger picture, which includes the good, joyful and positive too. However, gratitude isn't 'good' instead of 'bad': it's about recognising that there's a mixture of both good and bad available to us at any one time, even if the 'good' lies in the small things.

We can feel many things at once.

Be aware of when you might be using gratitude to shame yourself for normal feelings. We can feel many things at once. We are both light and dark in tandem, and one positive feeling need not negate a harder, sadder or crosser feeling. They can co-exist. I have to be aware of when I use a 'well, look on the bright side' attitude towards myself; it can be shaming behaviour that works to ignore and devalue my valid feelings. I am far more likely to do this when my self-esteem is low, as then I tend to use my emotions as a barometer of how good a person I am: envy, resentment, confusion, overwhelm make me a bad person; while happiness, gratitude, strength and energy make me a good one, right? No! We're an apothecary of all of these emotions, with constantly changing concoctions. We are light and dark, shiny and rough. That is the very nature of being human.

We can gaslight our emotions, devaluing and invalidating them with critical or abusive inner dialogue. For example, I might feel something and then tell myself: *That's ridiculous. Think of the good things in your life, and don't be selfish/ungrateful/rude/insensitive. I'm just making it up, I'm just being crazy. I shouldn't cry about this.* This sort of approach causes us to disrespect our own feelings and intuition, and to find ourselves questioning everything, such as whether or not we should be feeling or behaving in a certain way. We become conflicted within ourselves and lose confidence in being who we are. We judge ourselves harshly. The gap between what we feel we should be doing and thinking and feeling, and what we are actually doing and thinking and feeling, often becomes filled with shame, frustration and self-criticism. We can lessen this gap by trying to be kinder, more compassionate and realistic in what we expect of ourselves.

I love the word 'and'. It is a good reminder that we can feel many things at one time. Even though our feelings may seem conflicted, they can co-exist! Love doesn't mean that you cannot feel frustrated with the person you love. You can feel love and frustration. The one need not cancel out the other. You can feel love *and* frustration. You can feel gratitude *and* overwhelm. You can feel joy *and* depression. You can feel grateful *and* disappointed.

Because you people-please

I read emails through about ten times before I send them. It drives my colleagues mad but I'm so worried about anything I've said being taken the wrong way!

Lil

You are more likely to experience shame if you place a high value on the opinions – or perceived opinions – of others. If you let the thoughts and opinions of other people become statements of your worth and validity as an individual, that's a lot of power to give away. We're going to delve into the subject of people-pleasing in chapter 9, but I want to share an example here.

Say I was having a particularly stressful shopping trip with an overtired toddler. I see an older lady glance at me in disdain. I assume she is judging my parenting. If I were to take that as a statement of who I am, I would feel shame very quickly. Instead, I need to remind myself that her look is subjective, because her experience of me and my child is incredibly limited. She has not seen the bigger picture of our day. By putting such thoughts into context and coaching myself through the moment, I feel more able to let that wave of shame pass much more easily.

The lower your self-esteem, the more likely you are to look to the circumstances around you to get a gauge of your worth. But because those sources aren't actually very valid or accurate, the feedback you receive will most likely be skewed, thus nudging down your self-esteem even further. Remember this: failing doesn't make you a failure. Being disliked by someone doesn't make you unlikeable. Doing something 'bad' doesn't necessarily make you bad. And being misunderstood by someone doesn't make you impossible to understand.

How does shame impact your self-esteem?

I feel like I go into a relationship on the back foot. I'm waiting for him to realise I'm crap. My ex made me feel like nobody would ever love me.

Anonymous

Shame can be lonely and demoralising. It can become the background influencer in your life and your choices. It has a huge impact on your ability to experience joy and happiness, because those positive feelings are harder to embrace when you don't feel deserving of them.

Experiencing consistent shame can lead to social challenges too. If you're always looking for proof of the negative things you believe about yourself, you're more likely to invest in relationships and friendships that have unhelpful dynamics or toxic traits. This is because your self-esteem determines where you set the bar for your standards in your relationships. If you find it hard to believe that you are worthy of good, healthy and fulfilling relationships, it can be more challenging to seek them and keep them. Shame can lead to sexual difficulties too, because you need to feel safe in being vulnerable with the right person.

Shame can also impact your work life. You may feel like an imposter, waiting to be found out and proved unworthy of your responsibilities or position. It can lead to and fuel low self-esteem, depression and anxiety for all these reasons. The main reason is that you feel ashamed about who you are. This shame prevents you from enjoying being . . . you.

Just like guilt, shame can so easily keep us stuck. But if we begin to see shame as a red flag – there to point to something that needs to be addressed – we can act on it and free ourselves from its grasp. Getting to the root of shame can be life-changing. And therapy can be a really good context in which to explore it further if needs be. If you identify shame as a predominant cause of your low self-esteem, turn to Helpful Contacts, page 265, for guidance on where to find a counsellor.

How do you address shame?

I never realised how much my relationship with my older sister impacted my life now until I had counselling. I started to see things in a whole new light.

Anonymous

When you can begin to untangle what is and isn't your responsibility, or recognise the things to which you have been giving the power to dictate your self-esteem, you start to be more questioning when that familiar wave of shame rises up. As a therapist, lightbulb moments are one of my absolute favourite things. Once the light has been turned on in a situation, or a spotlight cast on a feeling that previously seemed unclear, we never see these things in the same way again. It invites potential for change. Remember the big old house? Until you stepped inside and turned the light on, you didn't know its potential, or what you'd need to do in order to enjoy that which was hidden under the dust.

Unfortunately, shame doesn't address itself. Only through finding clarity, and perhaps seeking support to untangle your past experiences, will it loosen its grip. If you don't address shame and guilt, you will forever live a life that tries to atone for it, deny it and hide from it . . . which is a majorly exhausting way to spend your precious time and energy.

But you *are* addressing it, because you're here reading this chapter and taking that first step.

Acknowledging and dealing with shame can feel like a bumpy ride. But if you have shame, it's already having an unpleasant impact on your life, regardless of how obvious it may be at first glance, and you deserve to live a life that isn't dictated by a feeling of being worthless. Because that is categorically untrue – you are not worthless.

Shame plays hide and seek

Shame likes to hide behind other, more familiar emotions. Shame might be hiding behind anger at someone or about something, or irritability or impatience at things that seem entirely disconnected from what you're ashamed about. For example, for many years I felt shame and worthlessness, and for a while, this shame would hide behind a drive to exercise in a way that wasn't kind to myself. I'd run 10 kilometres most days, ignoring illness or exhaustion. I wasn't exercising in order to strengthen my muscles or keep fit; the drive was one of cruel self-punishment.

By virtue of its very nature, shame likes to hide. Some of shame's favourite hiding places are behind addiction, anger, narcissism, self-harm and self-sabotaging behaviours. So keep an eye out for it. It's so easy to focus on addressing any habits that are harming you, rather than making sense of the shame that is fuelling the habits themselves.

To sum up

Acknowledge when you feel shame and guilt, and talk about it if you can. You continue to hold what you do not put down and, man, that stuff can sure get heavy! When you talk with someone about shame and guilt – be it a trusted friend, family member or therapist – and that person responds compassionately, shame loses some of its power. Like the vampire that flees from the light, shame and guilt cannot thrive around compassion. Talking things through helps you process them mentally and emotionally. It's like emptying out a box of jigsaw pieces, connecting a few pieces and placing the joined pieces carefully back in the box. The full picture might not have been revealed yet, but the pieces have shuffled and been seen for what they are.

There have been very significant moments in my life in which I've shared some of what have felt like my darkest, most shameful secrets. I remember the moment I shared something with a couple of friends that I had been struggling secretly with for years. I found it hard to formulate the words and for a good few moments, the sentences literally wouldn't even pass my lips. My ultimate fear, because I judged myself so harshly, was that my friends would judge me too. They didn't, but instead showed such kindness and compassion that this broke up my shame. Sometimes, we can only dismantle shame when we give ourselves the opportunity to welcome compassion into our most dark or hurt places. My friends' example of compassion helped me begin to show it to myself.

The roots of guilt and shame can spread deep and wide. This is why it is so vital to acknowledge their place in your life, so that you can reclaim the power they've held in determining your self-esteem.

JOURNAL POINTS

- How might you have been punishing yourself for things you haven't done wrong?
- How does shame feel in your body?
- What do you feel shame about? What is the underlying message about yourself that you have believed?
- How can you challenge those beliefs and bring some balance and compassion into them?
- Consider something you feel guilty for and apply the ACT technique: Address, Compassion, Tweak.

Chapter 7

Waging war on low self-worth: the thoughts

Mantra: *I am not what I think.*

I want to start with a question for you to consider. If you were to talk to your friends in the way you speak to yourself, using the same language and tone, would you have any friends left? The most important conversations you will ever have are the ones that no one else hears. It's those conversations that take place inside the secret silence of your mind, rarely pausing for breath. Imagine a radio that is stuck on, playing constantly at a low volume in your home. You may not always be consciously listening to the music, but you sometimes tune in to it as something catches your attention, or a song plays that you like. Occasionally, you find yourself humming songs that you didn't even realise had been playing earlier in the day. Even when you aren't listening consciously to the chatter inside your mind, aware of the words and tone, part of your brain is hearing it. It matters. It matters a lot.

Often when your self-esteem is low, your internal chatter tends to be quite critical, impatient, unforgiving, accusing, shaming and sometimes even bullying. We're going to find ways to change that. First, you must really get to know what your internal chatter sounds like (and maybe even 'who' it sounds like)! We're going to look at how this inner dialogue has been shaped and how it is holding you back. But, most importantly, I'm going to empower you to transform your internal dialogue into something that will help soften the peaks and troughs of your fluctuating self-esteem.

What is my internal dialogue?

Until I saw something about internal dialogue in your Mind Over Mother *book, I had no idea I had one, or how important it was. I was shocked at the things I say to myself. But now I have made it kinder and it has made such a difference!*

Tam

Your internal dialogue is that voice inside your head that sounds like you. It observes and comments on everything going on, both inside and outside of your mind. It makes sense of and extracts meaning from the world around you. It has observed everything from the moment you were born, so it's quite experienced. It knows you well and remembers even those things that your conscious mind has forgotten. It helps you make decisions and form opinions by applying experience, logic, rationality and reasoning to what's going on around you. It is shaped by the world around you, but it also shapes your understanding, perception and how you react to the world. Just as how you were treated as a child forms a benchmark for what you believed you were deserving of, the way you were spoken to becomes the blueprint for how you speak to yourself. Fortunately, this inner voice of yours can be changed, softened and made to become kinder, more patient and compassionate.

I first noticed my internal dialogue around the time my sister was diagnosed with cancer, when I must have been about five years old. I remember very clearly thinking that if anyone in my family died, it would be too painful. I'd simply have to die too. This came with some clear and shocking imagery in my mind, which I can still see now if I recall it. Such is the power of the mind and how things can imprint it and stay with us with sharp clarity some thirty years later. Only when I experienced depression in my early twenties, did I realise quite how cruel and powerful this internal dialogue had become.

Engaging in therapy helped me see very strong links between the words, tone and types of things my internal dialogue told me and the things that had actually been said to me in real life up to that point. I remember thinking how it was like I'd collected together all the (generally negative) things anyone had ever said, and was repeating them to myself, in various ways, in my head. Recognising that this dialogue was not actually me, even though it sounded exactly like my thoughts, was a game-changer. It took me a while to work out what actually was 'me' and what had been added to this constant stream of thoughts along the way. Once I did that, I could start to challenge and change those thoughts.

So, who am I then, if I am not my thoughts?

I am not my thoughts; I am the one observing them.

I am the one observing them. This light-bulb moment throws me every time, reminding me that the power lies with me and not in the thoughts I think. My thoughts change with my mood, experience, the day, my hormonal cycle, my energy levels. They change all the time, up and down, round and round, light and dark. My thoughts influence my feelings. If they are negative and critical, I feel low. If my thoughts are kind, forgiving and patient, I feel good. So, once I realised that I wasn't my thoughts, and that actually I could have power and control over them if I wanted to, I can also sometimes change my mood!

So, what is your internal dialogue? It is not you. Rather, you are the one observing it; that's who you are.

I'm not sure I have an inner voice

I think in pictures and feelings. And then I focus on one and then words come in. I know this probably sounds really strange, but I think that's my internal narrative.

Ibby

What happens when you drop things or stop rushing around? What goes on in your mind at night when you put your book down and switch off the light? What happens when you let your mind wander as you gaze out of the window; where does it go? Does it settle on a particular topic? Is it orientated in the past or the future, or does it sit in the present moment? Perhaps it flits between all three of those states? Not everyone has an internal narrative that sounds like a chatty, verbal dialogue. Your internal dialogue might be more of a feeling, or a stream of imagery, rather than a recognisable conversation whose words you can understand. Or it might switch between the visual and the verbal, or only become verbal when your attention is drawn to it. It runs automatically, informing your dreams both by day and night.

Regardless of whether your internal dialogue is more of a feeling, a conversation or reads like a comic book strip, what's important is what's being communicated. We can only change, challenge and control this internal narrative once we become aware of it. And that happens when we turn it into something comprehensible, which tends to mean using our own language; and this is why I call it the internal 'dialogue'.

I got my nose pierced a few months ago. For a while it surprised me every time I looked in the mirror. I could see the piercing out of the corner of my eye, often thinking it was a spot or a crumb – until I went to brush it away and felt a stab of pain! And now? Now it's just there. I barely even notice it anymore. It has become a part of who I am in a way, and my attention is only drawn to it when someone says, 'Oh Anna! You got your nose pierced', or asks me if it hurt! Our internal dialogue merges into the background of who we are; yet it is not who we are. Nevertheless, it impacts so, so much. You know how they often say that a murderer is someone the victim knew? The killer became a trusted part of the victim's life, so much so that they didn't see the threat. Your internal dialogue, the part of you that is so familiar, can so easily become a sort of background wallpaper you don't even 'see' any more. It can have a huge negative impact; yet it often goes unchecked, unchallenged and unquestioned.

How can internal dialogue be beneficial?

In and of itself, your internal dialogue is there to help you interact safely with, and make sense of, the world around you. It gives you the ability to formulate opinions, recognise feelings, reason with situations, and communicate your needs. If you have a good, helpful internal dialogue, it can act as your encourager, supporter, cheerleader and coach. It can parent you when you're having a hard day, being kind and encouraging you to reach out to others, or engage in positive coping mechanisms and techniques. If you have had the benefits of affirming caregivers during your childhood, you may have absorbed some of the kind things they said that made you feel supported, heard and helped. Those become your internal dialogue, forming a kind of internal support.

As a therapist, my hope is that my clients will absorb some of my own tone, compassion and insight into their own internal dialogue. My favourite thing to hear is when a client says, 'I was having a hard day and then your voice popped into my head and helped me find my way through it.' In the same way, although you may have internalised some of the negative ways people have spoken to you and treated you, you can choose to formulate kinder, more grounded and compassionate input too!

My internal dialogue has become much more kind and supportive over the years. Previously, if I was having a tough day I might say to myself: 'Oh, come on! Pull yourself together. Don't be stupid. You've got to be stronger than this.' Whereas now it might say: 'It's okay, Anna. You've felt like this before, it will pass. It always does. Breathe. Is there anything you need or someone you can talk to?' Of course, my inner voice is in no way perfect, and when I'm having a hard time, or I've deprioritised the things that keep me in a good headspace, my critical internal dialogue gains volume and power. I use this as a red flag to prompt me to explore my feelings and coping mechanisms.

What impact does my internal dialogue have on my self-esteem?

I've changed the way I speak to myself. Not all the time, but when I remember. For the first time, it was my birthday and I actually didn't want to run away from everyone who was kind to me.

Anonymous

What would it be like if you were to be followed around by a bully who repeatedly taunted you, pointing out your weaknesses and hurling a catalogue of your past failings at you every time you wanted to try something new? What would it be like if your childhood bully was still there beside you, like a shadow, everywhere you went? What would it be like if the person who had dismissed your feelings walked beside you, dismissing every feeling and need you had before you even got a chance to verbalise it? What if you had someone shining a light on your shame, guilt or feelings of unworthiness every time you dared to engage in something that made you feel happy and excited? What would that do to your self-esteem? What impact would it have on your confidence, your decision-making, your willingness to accept kindness and love or engage in things that made you happy?

By changing the soundtrack you live to, you can change your life.

This is what our internal dialogue can do. This is how powerful it can be. In many ways, while we can move on geographically and over time from those who've hurt, harmed or abused our vulnerability, we might have internalised their voice as part of how we speak to ourselves. How you speak to yourself dictates how you feel about your worth. And how you feel about your worth dictates how you speak to yourself. It's a bit 'chicken and egg', but the one feeds the other – and if needs be, the cycle must be stopped and reversed. By changing the constant soundtrack you live to, you can change your life. It may sound like an extravagant sales pitch, but it's true. I wouldn't say it if I hadn't seen it repeatedly in the lives of my clients, and in my own life as well. I'll be honest with you that it's not easy; in fact, for many of us, it needs to become a lifetime pursuit. But I promise it's worth your time and energy – and it is possible.

Get to know what needs changing

Last month I dropped a glass on the floor. I said, 'You idiot!' I sounded like my dad. And I realised that even though he'd died five years before, he was still alive in my head.

Anonymous

If your internal dialogue was a person, how would you describe that person? Would they be loud, angry, critical, funny, kind, slow, fast, accusatory, shy or resentful? Now I want you to think of some of the common words, feelings or phrases that you hear often in your mind. For me, at their worst, they would be: *you're stupid*; *a disappointment*; *angry, frustrated and irritated*; *grovelling to others*; *work harder, not good enough*. Now consider whether any of those tones, phrases or feelings remind you of anyone you've met throughout your life. It might even be an experience in which you felt a particular emotion such as fear, shame, embarrassment, being overlooked or ridicule, which has stuck with you because it was traumatic in some way.

We internalise the things that have been said to us. We are naturally trusting of those in positions of authority and responsibility when we are little. We don't question whether someone is right or wrong. If my parents told me that they made electricity

You are not your internal dialogue.

from candyfloss, I'd probably have believed them for a good while. Just as I believed a grey-bearded man flew in a sleigh around the world, delivering gifts at Christmas.

Now you've determined where some of the characteristics of your internal dialogue may have originated and how they have been integrated into this internal chatter of yours. Sure, these aspects might sound very much like you, but they are not you. And much of it is not true. You are not your internal dialogue. You are the one who observes it.

If you spoke to a child in the way your internal dialogue spoke to you, what would they grow up to believe about themselves? In many ways, knowledge really is power, and the more you remind yourself that your value is not the sum total of your thoughts, and you are not who your internal dialogue says you are, the more you can challenge and change what comes your way.

But my inner critic whips me into shape!

Let's face it, whilst perfectionism, drive, self-criticism and fear of what others think are pretty damn exhausting to hear day in and day out, they sometimes get you to good places. My perfectionism has meant that I've achieved things to a high standard. I ended up getting praised when working in advertising, because my fear of getting things wrong meant I was very meticulous. My drive and belief that my worth is a direct reflection of what I do has meant I get a lot done, pretty quickly. My concern about what people think has found me going out of my way to please them, and this has won me friends along the way; I'm sure of it.

So, surely my critical internal dialogue actually comes in handy? Yes, undoubtedly – but at a high cost. The cost is burnout, of striving, of giving myself away until all I have left are resentment and crumbs. Every compliment or thank you has fed my belief that doing, doing, doing (and doing well), is what makes me acceptable. It has driven my self-esteem into the ground and covered it in dust. It has taken me so far away from myself, that I've felt like an imposter in my own life, telling myself: *Sure, I'll say yes, and they'll be pleased with me. But if they knew how resentful/tired/frustrated/ empty/sad/grumpy I feel, they wouldn't like me ...*

So, yes, critical internal dialogue can drive you to success, friendship or brilliant work, but at what cost? And what is your true motivation? It's often fear. And how much joy can we feel in a life that has a constant undertone of fear of being found out, of failing, of being discovered to not be worthy? There wasn't much joy there for me, that's for sure.

Self-criticism isn't a good way to motivate yourself.

Self-criticism isn't a good way to motivate yourself. If I spoke to my children critically, they might do what I asked out of fear, but not out of honour or respect. I'd lose my connection with them, because they wouldn't feel that they were of worth to me if they were being constantly berated, criticised and having their flaws pointed out. When my four-year-old is acting out, he is far more likely to come out of a tantrum if I spend a moment trying to understand what led to it, and to comfort and listen to his feelings supportively, rather than shove him on the naughty step.

Imagine two teachers in a school. They each have their own class, and their students happen to get the same exam results.

Teacher 1: this teacher uses harsh discipline, dealing out detentions like sweets. She rules by fear, shouting in ears and standing over students with a cane, ready to rap the knuckles of any hands that make a mistake.

Teacher 2: this teacher is firm but gentle. He is confident, intuitive and listens to the students. If a child makes a mistake, he takes a moment to explain the correct answer and gives them another chance. He reassures his students that mistakes are simply opportunities to learn, and nobody is expected to get it right all the time.

Which class would you rather be in? The truth is that you can still get good results without bullying yourself.

The conclusions we draw and the statements we make

Someone once told me that becoming a singer was so competitive, I should find another thing to pursue. So I took a job in a cinema. I often wonder what would have happened if I had followed my heart instead.

Anonymous

When your self-esteem is low, you will place more value on the way people treat you and speak about you. If your self-confidence wavers, you are more likely to look to others for approval to gain that superficial spike of self-esteem. However, other people will *always* have a limited and flawed view of you, because they will always be looking at you through their own lenses and experiences.

Even someone who knows me well, and who says lovely things about me, has a limited and flawed view. No one else can ever fully 100 per cent see me and tell me 100 per cent who I am and how I am. Therefore I have to hold all other people's opinions loosely. Sure, I can draw from them, learn and let them change me; but I also need to remind myself that they are still just opinions. They don't change who I am and what I'm worth. Other people's opinions don't need to become part of my internal dialogue or the lens through which I view and understand the world.

How do I change my internal dialogue?

Here follows a pick–and–mix selection of tips and techniques to help you address your internal dialogue. Pick a couple that jump out for you and see what a difference they can make.

Little you

I often think about my younger self and what she needed. I try and give myself the support and kind words I needed back then.

Gi

I often encourage people to imagine speaking to a child in the way they speak to themselves. Usually, they recoil in horror at the mere thought. This technique can be quite powerful because of course you wouldn't want to speak to someone you value in such a critical way. But the fact of the matter is, if it's not good enough for another person or a little child, it's not good enough for you either.

To try out this technique, find a photograph of yourself as a child, or, if you don't have a physical photo, conjure up an image of 'little you' in your mind. Look 'little you' in the eyes. Remember how it felt to be her, what she used to feel and how she used to see the world. I'm hoping you'll have a sense of compassion for that younger you.

Imagine speaking to that child in the way that you speak to yourself today. Whenever you find yourself speaking critically to yourself or with a bullying, unforgiving or impatient tone, recall or look at that image of 'little you', and attempt to amend the words and tone you are using to those that would feel more appropriate.

Now, one day, a photo of you as you are now will become the 'little you' of a much older you. And I bet older you, with her additional experience, insight and retrospect, would want to tell you to be kind to yourself today. You are very likely doing the best you can, with the knowledge and experience you have.

Name your internal dialogue

I call my critical voice Trevor because I had an angry uncle called Trevor. I call my kind voice 'Nancy' because in my mind she's like a caring, older lady who looks like my nan, Nancy. She's always there.

Amelia

Sometimes it can be helpful to turn your internal dialogue into a person by using a name and imagining how they may look. This can be a good reminder that your critical internal chatter is not who you are.

Set a new tone

I imagine what my mum would say when I'm having a tough moment. I literally used to call her every day, but now it's like she's in my head. I'm pretty sure she's relieved not to have so many phone calls!

Evan

You've spent time considering the tone of your internal dialogue. It's time now to find an internal cheerleader. Think of how you'd support and cheer on a friend, wanting to offer a helpful perspective when they're beating themselves up. Often this is because we find it much easier to apply worth and compassion to other people's situations and emotions than we do to our own. So think about people in your life who are kind and compassionate. If you can't think of a specific individual, make someone up! When you notice your critical dialogue pick up, consider what this kind person might say or how they might support you. Imagine them there beside you, providing confident and affirming reassurance to guide you through whatever you are facing.

The other day I got sick. I had intended to write another 2,000 words of my book yet there was no chance of even looking at my laptop. My internal dialogue immediately jumped to the negative and the critical: *Anna, come on! You're not going to meet your own deadline, you're such a failure. Always setting targets too high so that you fall at the last hurdle.* If I'd have listened to this critic, I'd have felt even more disheartened and my self-esteem would have dipped. So I chose to imagine a kinder, compassionate dialogue (which, after practice, is increasingly accessible to me and quick to rush to my rescue), telling myself: *These things happen, it's okay. Move some bits about next week and you can catch up! You always do. Now, get some help for the kids if you can, and rest.* The compassionate voice wasn't invalidating my feelings of frustration but acknowledging them and reminding me that I am only human, comforting me like a kind friend or parent. It brought some welcome balance to my black–and–white thinking of: *Oh, it's all gone to pot, I always do this.*

Pause and consider what your internal dialogue is saying to you. Even if you don't believe the kind words you are using to counteract it, use them regardless. The 'counter' voice should be compassionate, kind, patient, forgiving and encouraging. I don't doubt that you find it easy to exhibit many of those qualities towards those you care about, so now turn them in towards yourself.

Question the generalisations you make about yourself

My husband always called me 'highly strung'. I thought that was who I'd become as I'd gotten older. However, we went on holiday and I changed as a person. It made me question whether I was just stressed and overwhelmed. Now I see being 'highly strung' as a red flag telling me that I need to de-stress, rather than accept it as part of who I am.

Be wary of the statements you make about yourself.

Sadie

Be wary of the statements you make about yourself. We tend to see things through the lens of our self-esteem, so if your self-esteem is low you are more likely to veer towards negative statements and not to question them. This means you are more vulnerable to cognitive distortions. Cognitive distortions occur when your self-esteem distorts the facts of reality, and your thoughts become more critical and upsetting. Just because you feel abandoned or rejected doesn't mean you aren't worthy of acceptance. If you don't challenge the belief that you deserve abandonment and rejection, you are more likely to abandon or reject yourself in little ways. This might take the form of ignoring your own feelings, needs and opinions, and not seeking support when you need it.

If something bad happens, a generalisation might be that 'the world is a bad place'. Of course, bad things happen in the world – but also good things happen too. Gratitude can be helpful in addressing this attitude by drawing our attention away from ruminating on what is going wrong or could go wrong, to what is going right. It's not about ignoring our fears or emotions, but bringing balance to them and reminding ourselves that not everything is bad. Some of my generalisations are:

- I'm rubbish at directions.
- I'm impatient.
- I'm anxious.
- I am not a good enough mother.
- I'm terrible at spelling and grammar.
- Driving is dangerous.
- I always burn stuff when I cook.

Find a way to bring some flexibility into these generalising statements, so they don't sound quite so factual. Some of these statements have had an incredible amount of power when, really, they are just opinions. Here is what happens when I make my generalising statements a little more balanced and flexible:

- I'm rubbish at directions:

I like to use the sat nav as I can't always rely on my memory of routes I've not done often.

- I'm impatient:

When I'm tired, I can feel impatient.

- I'm anxious:

I sometimes have anxious thoughts so I've got good tools and techniques to use.

- I am not a good enough mother:

I love my kids and they love me. I do my best – nobody is perfect and they don't need a perfect mother!

- I'm terrible at spelling and grammar:

I love to write, and am very creative with my use of words. I am also very grateful for spellcheck!

Question the generalisations other people make about you

Words can be the balm you need; they can encourage, comfort and build you up. They can change your life: *Will you marry me?* They can redirect your path: *Would you like the job?* But they can also have a huge impact on your confidence and the way you live.

> *Kids at my tennis class always used to say I was crap. It affected my confidence for years. Recently I've started playing again. I know I'm not amazing, but I enjoy it and that's the important thing.*
>
> Flavia

An empowering thing to do is to remember that you can take the words of others and choose how much value you want to apply to them. Instead of just letting them hop on the boat without questioning them, you can actually decide whether you want to take them on board. Maybe you need to add some context or rationality to them first.

Here are some statements I've been told that went unquestioned by me for many years:

- You're ugly.
- You're not funny.
- You're stupid.
- You aren't academic.
- You're annoying.

These things were some of the statements uttered to me in

childhood. Maybe as jokes, maybe as part of a wider context that I didn't quite understand at the time. Either way, they formed part of how I understood myself. Surely if that's what people saw, it must be true? Or so I thought. These statements impacted how I entered new classrooms, schools and jobs, and how I tackled new experiences. I would try to compensate for my perceived lack by attempting to be whatever I thought would make me more likeable at the time. I don't know whether it was my own therapy or my training that made me start to challenge these statements. I began to question the validity of them and ponder on the mindset of the people who spoke them to me. The very act of questioning what for so long had felt like truth, was a turning point.

Perhaps what other people say isn't always true. Perhaps what you say about yourself isn't always true either. Now there *is* a truth.

Recognise the 'when x, then x' approach

I run my own business and always tell myself that I can slow down when I've got another client. But I'm realising it's counterproductive. All I do is collapse into a heap because I'm trying so hard. I do much better when I allow myself to step away and recharge.

Philippa

I don't know about you, but this is a big one for me! My internal chatter will often say something like this: *When I've hit 10,000 words today, then I'll relax. When I've tidied the whole house, then I can have a bath.* Now, this approach is not a bad technique to use to motivate yourself, but be wary of what goals you are setting and what the rewards are. If the rewards are actually essential things for your mental wellbeing, such as rest, relaxation, slowness and connection, then how kind is it to make yourself work so hard for what should be a basic human right? Sure, work hard, but find small ways to rest along the way. We shouldn't work in order to earn rest; we should rest in order to work productively.

Be wary of comparison

I drive this old banger. I can't afford to get it fixed up. Everywhere I go, I fixate on other people's cars and it makes me feel like I've somehow failed at life.

Anonymous

Comparing yourself to others is an act of self-disrespect.

Comparing yourself to others is an act of self-disrespect. There will always be someone whom you consider to be better or worse off than yourself in various aspects of your life and abilities. Everyone has light and dark sides. Everyone has hidden depths and unknowns. Become mindful of when you are comparing one person's outward expression, behaviour or curated reel of highlights to your behind-the-scenes reality. It's never going to be a fair comparison because you don't know the full picture. You never will.

When you notice you are engaging in comparison, ask yourself why you are comparing yourself to someone else: what has motivated you and what are you hoping to find evidence of? Whether you're looking to find proof of a failing or a success, looking outside yourself for validation is at best sketchy!

Affirmations

> *I underestimated mantras for years until I heard someone saying 'you aren't your thoughts'. And it stayed with me.*
>
> Noor

I have included a mantra in each chapter of this book because I personally find them so useful and thought you might too. They can cut through the buzz of my mind and act like little anchors to hold me secure amidst a storm of thoughts. In fact, so powerful was the metaphor of an anchor for me, that I had one tattooed on my wrist as a constant reminder! Mantras can offer a productive thought of clarity, reminding you to be more present in the now.

The important thing is that you find a mantra easy to remember and recall. It needs to be helpful when you need it most. Pick one, note it down, memorise and repeat. Or switch it up when you need something slightly different. Some of my own favourites include:

- I am not my thoughts.
- I am deserving of good things.
- My worth is fixed.
- Speak to myself as someone I care about.
- Comparison is the thief of joy.
- I accept myself for who I am.

- I will anchor myself in the truths I know.
- I choose a kinder thought.
- I am thankful for what I can do.
- This moment matters.

Meditate

Meditation has become a part of my daily life now. It helps slow my mind when I'm trying to go to sleep. It has become a still place in my mind I can return to when I want.

Anonymous

Meditation offers an opportunity to quiet a turbulent, active mind. You know how when it's so noisy, it's hard to think? The other day, I realised that when I'm reversing the car, or having to focus in another way, I immediately turn off the radio. Meditation aims to calm some of the background noise so that you can gain inner clarity, focus and control.

I particularly like guided meditation, and often practise it for ten minutes a day using an app or a free online video. Some types of meditation encourage you to use a mantra or a simple chant, which you can return to whenever you notice your mind whizzing off somewhere (for me, it's often thinking about what to add to the shopping list or cobble together for dinner). Internal dialogue often focusses on the past (what we should have done), or the future (what we should do). So meditation can be really helpful in drawing our mind back to the present, where the real living is. This is where you are; this is your only reality; this moment will never come again. Meditation helps you to develop the skill of being more present.

I want to say here that meditation is not suitable for everyone, especially if you have gone through trauma that rears its head as soon as you are still or quiet. If you recognise this to be the case, I recommend trauma therapy in order to help process what you've been through so that you can reclaim your headspace back.

Gratitude

It took my brother nearly dying to make me realise how important it is not to take the little things for granted.

Fari

I've touched on this in a very small way earlier in this book, but gratitude can be such a powerful tool when trying to inject some positivity, acceptance, presence and hope in our minds. I remember a conversation I had with family over Christmas 2019. My mum said to my sister-in-law and my husband, 'I have never seen Anna so content.' Now, considering this was quite a chaotic time in my life, with three young kids to look after, she was absolutely right. I just hadn't realised anyone else had noticed. All that had changed was that I had begun to practise gratitude.

It all began with a very simple tweak in language a year before. It sounds a bit over the top, but I'm pretty sure it changed my life. I'm not even sure how it happened or how I thought of it. Whether I saw it on the internet or suggested in the pages of a book or magazine. But I remember that I was unloading the washing machine, in a bit of a grump about the relentless stream of dirty laundry that I deal with. Suddenly, 'Ugh, I've got to do the washing' turned into 'I get to do the washing'. I get to do the washing ... in a washing machine I am so lucky to have access to; in a home that keeps us safe; of clothes that keep us warm and which we were able to purchase; for my kids and husband, who I love. Suddenly the mundane became the remarkable and I found myself with tears in my eyes, startlingly aware of my own privilege.

Now, I'm not saying I wander around in a perpetual state of wonder today, with butterflies dancing round my head, but this simple tweak has been transformative in those moments when I find my thoughts fixated on the negative, or I'm marching around the house huffing about all that hasn't been done. It turns my attention from focussing on what has gone wrong, or could go wrong, to acknowledging what has gone right and is going right.

However, as mentioned in chapter 6, it's important that gratitude is used to bring balance and light into darkness, rather than used to shame yourself for your very valid and normal feelings. It's okay that certain aspects of life feel relentless and annoying! But you can feel grateful and privileged at the same time! For so long, I didn't acknowledge that I could feel irritated *and* grateful simultaneously, and that one feeling need not negate the other! We can feel multiple things at once.

Have a quick debate

It started feeling like I was picking fights with myself, but then the nicer 'fighter' became stronger and louder, and the mean one started to back down a bit more.

Anika

Have you ever rehearsed an important conversation to make sure you feel confident in getting your point across? You might play out both sides of the argument in your head, imagining how the other party might respond or what they might say. Well, sometimes your internal dialogue can feel like a two-sided debate. In fact, as you start to challenge it, it can often feel like you are arguing with a part of yourself!

As mentioned earlier, I often encourage clients of mine to start overriding their critical dialogue with a more compassionate voice (see page 143). However, sometimes this voice can be hard to believe – especially when your belief system has been dominated by the critical things you tell yourself. It can feel like it turns into a bit of an argument, or a power struggle. As you become more confident and quicker at bringing in a kinder voice, it's like strengthening a muscle. It gains volume and clout.

To sum up

Changing your internal chatter is a learning process and it will take a while to address the habits of a lifetime! But honestly, it's so worth it. You won't always be successful, but if you start by managing at least one positive internal response a day, then that's one more time you've not been internally bullied. That's incredibly positive! You will see progress little by little. If you nudge the flight path of a plane by a few degrees, it can end up in a different continent – just like these small tweaks can change the course of your life and bring your self-esteem to a more stable place. Trust me, you'll feel differently about yourself when you aren't living to the background buzz of self-criticism.

If you notice your internal dialogue get a little crueller, ask yourself what's going on. Is there anything that has challenged your self-esteem recently? Are you more tired than normal? Could it be your hormones that are using some of your extra resources? We need energy to address our internal dialogue, as it requires focus and attention.

JOURNAL POINTS

- What are the three characteristics that describe your internal dialogue?
- Does your internal dialogue remind you of anyone you've encountered in life?
- If you spoke to a child in the way you speak to yourself, how would it impact their self-esteem?
- What are some of the costs of listening to your inner critic?
- Write down a list of fifty things that you're grateful for. See how your mood shifts.

Chapter 8

Continuing the war on low self-worth: the actions

Mantra: *I treat myself with respect.*

Words without actions are, well, just words really. Words can be helpful, but without actions to back them up, they start to lose their power. You can stand in the mirror and repeat loving mantras to yourself over and over. It might challenge your thinking for a while, but unless you begin treating yourself accordingly, those phrases will soon become water off a duck's back. I could tell my kids I love them a hundred times per day, but unless I'm treating them with care and respect, my words will soon mean very little indeed. They will feel like empty statements. Actions don't just back up words; they speak louder than them. Whilst 'I love you' is very nice to hear, if we treat someone with love, they'll feel loved regardless of how many times we say it.

Often, we experience a double whammy: our internal dialogue is critical and, without realising it, our actions towards ourselves amplify and compound its criticisms, making them even more powerful. So, now you're started to take steps to address your internal dialogue, it's important that you also take steps to start changing the way you behave towards yourself. Self-care is often seen as being a bit cheesy, so we are going to 'de-cheese' self-care in this chapter! We'll look at exactly what it is, what it isn't, how it fits into the bigger picture of how we treat ourselves, and why addressing it is a vital part of working on self-esteem. You are worthy of having your feelings validated and your needs met, but first you need to know what these are. This chapter will also explain how to climb off the exhausting burnout rollercoaster that low self-worth has us firmly sat upon. You deserve rest – and I'm going to have you daring to believe it.

Reframing self-care

I didn't really want to mention self-care at first, because I know the phrase initiates the odd eye-roll. It conjures up saccharine images of having a nice, long bath while wearing a face mask, or taking a spa break. Many of us have begun to label the cornerstones of mental health, such as rest, hydration and good nutrition, as 'self-care'. We've turned what should be non-negotiables into indulgent, optional treatments.

However, the more I think about self-care, talk about it and write about it, the more my understanding about what exactly self-care is changes. I'm going to break 'self-care' down further in this chapter so we can start to think about it in a different way. Instead of looking at self-care as a catch-all term, we're going to explore it as part of the bigger picture around the way you treat yourself, and look at:

- Self-preservation
- Self-respect
- Self-care
- Self-love

Self-preservation – head down and carry on

Everyone sees me as super busy, juggling work, the dogs and the foster kids. Nobody would believe I have these times where I just cry and feel horrendous. Then I pick myself back up, and get back out there.

Anonymous

To me, self-preservation is that basic state in which we focus on preserving our own existence. Self-preservation is those moments in life when you've been faced with a challenge and have powered on through. Perhaps you needed to ignore physical exhaustion so that you could care for a sick relative. Maybe you had to put aside your own fear so that you could comfort someone younger and more vulnerable than yourself. We hear stories of people finding apparently superhuman strength to lift cars off people, and to act in ways and at speeds they'd never usually be able to in moments of challenge or trauma – which draw on the same sort of energy.

The thing is that while our self-preservation response is there to keep us safe and alive, it should never be a physical state in which we have to live for extended periods of time. Yet many people do! I, for one, have spent lots of time in a heightened state designed to preserve my life, not be my life. I have felt constantly on edge, with my emotions just below the surface. I seemed like I was fine, but I wasn't thriving; I was surviving. When people ask me how I managed during one of the hardest times of my life, I say I had no choice. I wasn't 'living'; I was moving through life like a machine – not engaging, laughing, loving or living; just doing and going through the necessary motions.

You too might find yourself on a rollercoaster of stress and burnout; living in a way that has you functioning at a stressed or anxious level. If you ignore the warning signs – the little red flags that say, 'Hey, I need a rest. Please slow down' – then you too may experience your own sort of emotional meltdown. This is very common for those whose self-esteem is attached to the principle of 'do, do, do'.

When you're living in such a heightened state of self-preservation, you are likely doing the bare minimum when it comes to really caring for yourself. You may be meeting your basic needs just enough to keep carrying on. Your feelings are likely to be pushed aside to allow you to focus on the task at hand, which consumes all your reserves and leaves you scraping the bottom of the energy barrel. You may find you have little energy for fun, being present, being excited or happy; for laughter and relaxation. You might feel irritable and anxious as your whirling thoughts demand energy that you don't quite have available right now. You may also find it harder to sleep even though you're exhausted, because when you slow down for bedtime, your feelings and fears rush to the forefront of your mind, making it harder for you to switch off. There is little regard for your own needs, feelings, opinions and passions, because your focus is on facilitating those of the people around you, or just making it through each day.

Self-respect

When I realised I'd gotten into the habit of not drinking a drop of water until the evening, I knew something had to change.

Barbs

Let's unpick the idea of self-respect a little bit, because many of us aren't actually giving it to ourselves. Respect is the way most of us would treat a stranger, acknowledging them as a fellow human being of value. You wouldn't necessarily roll out the red carpet for them, but you'd respect their need for space, and you wouldn't ignore them if they wound the window of the car down to ask for directions. What would that stranger think you thought of them, if you treated them in the way that you treat yourself?

Self-respect is so important in order to lift our low self-esteem to a healthier place. When you respect yourself as an individual – a human with needs, wants, flaws and limitations – it impacts the decisions you make, how you use your resources and where you place your boundaries. Self-respect asks you to value your own needs. To take up your space in the world; for you are as deserving of space, physically and verbally, as anyone else. Consider your basic needs: food, water, warmth, safety, purpose, creativity, human connection and relationships are the main ones. These things are not about self-care: they are self-respect. They are not about rolling out the red carpet, but about acknowledging your humanity. Here are some simple acts of self-respect:

- Washing
- Taking prescribed medication
- Going to bed at a sensible time
- Brushing your teeth
- Using the toilet when you need to
- Wearing warm clothes when it's cold
- Eating nourishing food when you are hungry
- Drinking enough water
- Asking for support when you need it
- Asserting a boundary in a relationship
- Verbalising your needs

These acts represent the cornerstones of good mental health. They are priorities, the fundamental building blocks upon which your day should be based. Oh, the number of times I've needed a wee and then spent ages hopping desperately around the kitchen, when the loo was in eyeshot. Instead, I've prioritised unloading the dishwasher, grabbing yet another snack for a hungry toddler, or answering an email. Going to the loo when I need a wee doesn't need to be seen as an act of self-care, but of self-respect. Self-respect is about going to bed at a time that acknowledges your need for rest and your current energy levels; whereas self-care is going to bed early, lighting a candle and picking up a book.

Self-respect encourages you to take responsibility for your own behaviour and choices and their repercussions. When a decision is made out of a place of self-respect and healthy boundaries, our self-respect encourages us to hold our hands up if things do go awry, feel the disappointment and move on. When you respect yourself in a positive way, you'll naturally invite respect from those around you too.

You're worthy of respect.

When you don't respect yourself, you are dehumanising yourself. You are telling yourself that you are unique in your lack of worth. Everyone has the same value, yet, somehow, you believe you are the one that slipped through the net. You are not the exception to the rule that all human beings are worthy of respect and of having their basic needs met. You are not the one whose flaws are unforgivable, whose failings make you unlovable. When we say we are not worthy of respecting our own needs, boundaries and emotions, we are rejecting a fundamental fact that *everybody* is worthy of these things. You are just as worthy as anyone else. Sure, it may not feel true, but it is true. Feelings aren't facts. Facts are facts. You're worthy of respect. From others. From yourself. Fact.

Self-care

I work for my dad and he lets me come in a bit late one morning a week so I get to the pool early. He sees how happy it makes me and I'm way happier in the office because of it.

Zeena

Now, if meeting your basic needs is actually about self-respect and self-preservation, then self-care is the next step. It's kindness. It's the gift you give yourself and an acknowledgement of your worth.

Sure, I can meet the basic needs of a guest who comes to stay. I can ensure that she is fed and watered and has somewhere safe to sleep. That is about respect; while care manifests itself in the rolled towel on the bed and the water on the bedside table. It's the offer of breakfast in the morning and the purchase of some juice and croissants because I know she will like them. I've stepped it up from the minimum required, and made extra effort. How is my guest likely to feel? Touched, appreciated, wanted. If self-respect is the shower, self-care is the long bath with the book.

Self-care builds self-esteem, which is the lens through which we view our immovable worth.

Self-care builds self-esteem, which is the lens through which we view our immovable worth. So be sure to meet your basic needs and then go beyond them, because there will be other things that you know are important for your personal wellbeing beyond being fed and watered. These are the things that acknowledge your individuality and which make you feel happy and fulfilled. They energise you in some way and make you feel alive. For me, self-care is about going out for walks in woodland with a friend, chatting on the sofa with a glass of wine in hand, or wandering through a small town that I've never visited before. It's having a bath with a facemask and properly drying my hair afterwards. It's running through fields instead of doing a perfunctory fifteen minutes of jumping around indoors in the name of exercise. Those things are extras, and they make me feel good. They refuel me more than a glass of water and an early bedtime. They give me a spring in my step and a sparkle in my eye. That is self-care to me.

How much of this kind of self-treatment do you engage in? And how does that stack up to the amount of time and energy you spend encouraging this kind of feeling for others?

Self-love

Sometimes I can confidently say I love myself. Not in a big-headed way.

Christa

Self-love is a term that gets batted around quite a lot, especially on social media. I don't want you to put pressure on yourself to aim for this right now. As we know full well, love isn't something we can force; it's something that grows over time when nurtured.

Do I love myself? Sometimes, maybe. I'm moving towards that, which is a far cry from the self-hatred I used to feel almost constantly. When I think about love and the love I feel for my family, whilst the love is constant, the feelings fluctuate. Sometimes my husband is annoying, sometimes I am not nice to be around, and sometimes it feels like my kids are on a mission to push me beyond my limits; and yet I know I love them.

Love isn't a simple or straightforward feeling. Love is sometimes a decision to act lovingly even though you don't feel loving. That's how relationships work; otherwise we'd bail out as soon as that starry-eyed feeling softens and recedes. I don't feel that starry-eyed towards myself; but the more compassion I find for myself when needed, and the kinder I am towards myself, the more this nurtures that loving acceptance of myself.

Know your needs

Honestly? I don't even know what I need.

Manuela

If you are going to begin to meet your own needs more often, it's important you know what they are! Here, I'm talking your physical, emotional, mental and spiritual needs – all your needs! I ask pretty much all my clients a deceptively simple question: 'Tell me three things you need.' This is almost always followed by a contemplative pause. Sometimes tears come as they try to formulate a response.

The tears acknowledge quite how hard it is to consider their own needs.

You may have overlooked your own needs for so long that you don't even know what they are anymore. Perhaps you've brushed them under the carpet, beaten them down with the gratitude stick, compared them away or diminished them. Maybe your focus is often on the needs of others instead. My own mind is a constant buzz of monitoring the needs of those around me, especially my kids. Are they thirsty? Do they need a snack, a nap, a break? Am I good enough for them? But even before kids, my mind would be buzzing all the time with similar thoughts: *Am I annoying my colleague? Am I being too loud, too quiet, too much or not enough? Do I need to make them another drink, are they bored, shall I offer to help? Am I taking up too much space on this train seat? Am I a burden on that friend?* This is because – and it may be the same for you too – my understanding of how acceptable I was, was tightly intertwined with how useful I believed I was in the world.

To be able to meet your needs, you need to know what they are. Ask yourself as you would a friend or child: 'Can I help you? What do you need?' Sometimes you have to take this question outside of yourself somehow, and asking yourself a direct question can get you thinking in a slightly different way. Try on feelings and emotions like clothes, and see what fits. Sometimes, when I'm not sure how I feel or what I need, I make a mental list of my possible emotions or needs. Am I angry, hurt, tired, overwhelmed, stressed, sad? Do I need support, space, company, lunch? One of these might jump out to me. As you become more attentive and gentle towards yourself, you will find it easier to recognise what needs and feelings have arisen for you. And then you can try to meet them.

Parent yourself

Sometimes I feel like I'm being my own parent, and this can be an incredibly helpful tactic. Because this is really what we need to do at times. None of us is one-dimensional: there is a part of us that wants to take the easy route, whatever that may be. It's the same part of me which, this morning, had me arguing with my grown-up self that I didn't want to get out of bed. I didn't want to go downstairs and make breakfast. I wanted to laze and watch boxsets in my pyjamas. But my grown-up self acknowledged my tiredness, whilst reminding me of my responsibilities. She ushered me out of bed and downstairs.

However old we are, we all have this younger, hidden part of ourselves: our inner child. If we have been parented in an ideal way, we can also shape our upbringing into an inner parent and use its kind, firm yet loving voice to coax our inner child in the right direction. If you didn't have that **Thoughts aren't facts.** sort of parenting, you will need to create your inner parent by yourself. This inner adult can encourage you to take steps that will increase your self-esteem.

Occasionally, when my self-worth is low, my inner child will kick up a storm in a similar way to how my kids some-times behave – with black-and-white feelings and thoughts that lack rationality and clarity: *What's the point? Nobody gets me, I'm no good, I'm a failure, I'm unlovable.* My inner parent will remind me that those are just my thoughts. Thoughts aren't facts. I'm liked by those important to me, and worthy of being treated with respect. My thoughts can change my behaviour. If I feel like a bad person, my inner child will argue, why get up and do a workout that I know will make me feel good? If I feel 'bad' about myself, I'm less motivated to do the things that are good for me. That's when my inner parent steps in: 'Come on, Anna. I know you feel rubbish, but we also know that getting outside really helps you when you feel like this. You're worthy of feeling good.' This is how closely entangled your inner dialogue and your behaviour are; addressing one helps you to address the other.

Don't wait until you feel worthy

I used to do dance as a teenager and loved it. I always said I'd do it again as it gave me so much enjoyment, but I kept putting it off for when I'd have more time. A friend asked me to go with her. It made me feel so good. I wish I hadn't waited so long.

Franki

One whacking great, enormous brick wall that often blocks us from treating ourselves with respect, is that it's tempting to wait until we feel like we're 'worth it' before we begin to implement nurturing habits. The truth is that if I'd waited until I felt worthy of good things, before I sought them out or accepted them into my life, I'd still be waiting. This is partly because my thoughts and feelings fluctuate like the British summer weather, but also because my actions change my self-esteem as much as my self-esteem changes my actions. If I waited until I felt worthy of treating myself kindly, I could be waiting forever.

Love is a choice, a decision.

I went to a wedding once, and the lady leading the sermon said something that has stayed with me all these years later: 'Love isn't always a feeling, it's a decision.' She was, of course, telling the newlyweds that they may not always feel that starry-eyed, loved-up feeling, because that changes. Love is a choice, a decision. I can be annoyed with my husband, yet still choose to do the loving thing of talking it out, offering an olive branch, forgiving or apologising.

This feels very relevant when talking about self-worth. Just like love is a decision, treating yourself as someone of worth, in order to grow your self-esteem, is a decision that needs to override any fluctuating emotions. I've realised recently that when I'm tired or hormonal, I somehow feel worth less. My inner critic leaps loudly into action and my behaviour follows suit. It takes energy to coach myself out of that loop, but it's a decision.

Sometimes the best decisions involve doing the things we least want to do when we least want to do them. I doubt every Olympic athlete rolls out of bed at unearthly hours on dark winter mornings, wanting to rush out and go train-ing. If they waited until they felt like an athlete in order to act like one, it would never happen. It's the bigger-picture thinking that drives them – the growth, the building of strength and stamina. Muscle fibre by muscle fibre. Ice bath by ice bath, day by day, session by session. That medal isn't just a celebration of a time beaten, but of those thousands of decisions made over feelings. It's about the legs swung out of bed into track shoes, when the feelings say 'stay'. Your self-esteem will grow each time you choose self-respect over criticism, kindness over cruelty, compassion over shame.

Emotional comparison

I tell myself to look on the bright side. I feel guilty when I feel low because others have it harder than me.

Anonymous

Emotional comparison has been such a big issue for me, and now that I've recognised how freely I compare my emotions, I notice it all the time in others too. I wrote this book amidst a global pandemic, where everyone was adrift on the same sea, facing a global storm of uncertainty, but sitting in very different boats. Undoubtedly, some of us had it harder, sadder and scarier than others. Some people lost loved ones, and some spent eye-wateringly long shifts on the medical frontlines, sweating behind gowns and masks. Some lost jobs, incomes, everything 'normal'. Some, like me, spent weeks cooped up safely at home, with a garden and a regular online shopping delivery. Yet I still experienced overwhelm, fear, anxiety and uncertainty. How dare I feel these emotions? I was not mourning; I was not on the medical frontline; I was not alone; I was not desperately trying to work out how on earth to feed our family.

Feelings are feelings. End of story. If you feel them, they are real to you. And if they are real, they have value. You don't need to dissect them, analyse them or swim around in them. You don't need to compare them, shame them, shut them down or diminish them. Just acknowledge the feeling, let it be and it will move through you.

Acknowledge the feeling, let it be - and it will move through you.

If you use other people's circumstances to guilt-trip yourself out of a feeling, you shove your emotion behind a wall. It doesn't go anywhere, it doesn't go away; it just gets hidden. Feelings are waves: they come and go, ebb and flow, rise and fall, all on their own. You don't need to mess with the process by beating yourself over the head with the positivity stick every time you feel a feeling you don't want to feel: *I shouldn't feel sad because x has it worse than me.* Someone else will always have it better or worse than you. Always. That feeling is there regardless of whether you want to feel it or not, or how appropriate you believe it to be. Let it be and it will move.

I don't know about you, but for a long time I grouped emotions into 'good' and 'bad'. Like some kind of distorted emotional diet. Good emotions included happiness, gratitude, forgiveness, love, patience and kindness; while the bad ones were anger, sadness, hurt, resentment, frustration and irritation. I could have as much as I liked of the good emotions, but should try to skimp on the bad ones. And if I binged on bad emotions, I would feel guilt and shame.

Now, as with food choices, you know that the healthiest way to live is to allow nothing to get out of bounds, but to seek balance and enjoy the variety of tastes and textures. It's the same with emotion: a bit of everything is more than acceptable, it's sustainable, human and healthy. Someone else's sadness doesn't make your sadness any less sad, either. Sadness is sadness. If you want to acknowledge someone else's circumstances, allow them to inspire a sense of gratitude.

Your emotions aren't everything – they won't even always make much sense – but they are *your* emotions; and devaluing, shaming and invalidating them means devaluing, shaming and invalidating *yourself*. Accepting who you are means accepting all that you are, even if you'd like to address, grow, strengthen or change some of it.

Stepping off the burnout rollercoaster

One day, I said, 'I can't' and they were still my friend. That was when I started acknowledging that I couldn't do it all and be happy.

Tara

You are not what you do. If you live as if your value is the sum of how much you do and give out, you will win a ticket to the burnout rollercoaster. This is not a sustainable way to live, because constantly giving out completely ignores your human nature: the fact that you have limited resources, and that you need to be nurtured, refuelled and supported too.

For me, this sort of overwhelm often looks like a full diary, with a lot of yeses and a smiling, sociable face. And then, depleted and behind closed doors, I become low, irritable, resentful and self-critical, and I want to retreat. Everyone gets the best of me – apart from me (although my family don't really enjoy my burnt-out, resentful self either)! This resentment is toxic. It's a sign that I've agreed to take on more than I have the resources to fulfil, and that I haven't restocked my resources enough. It can leave me feeling hurt by those who have actually done little more than ask something of me. They don't know my bigger picture; they can't see my diary, my energy levels, my limits. Only I can; therefore it is my responsibility to put those boundaries in place.

I once had a colleague who, when asked if he could help out at an evening event, would give a simple answer: a yes or no. Neither reply came with any explanations or apologies. It would often rile me when his 'no' came without an *I'm so sorry, I'd love to, I feel really bad that I can't* . . . But if I really think about it, my irritation came tinged with envy. I was jealous that he didn't feel the need to justify himself. His 'no' could have been because he had an important appointment that evening, or simply because he needed a night at home on the sofa with his partner. Yet, whilst sometimes inconvenient, I admired his confident 'no'. I'd be the person saying 'yes', despite my circumstances, and then feeling resentful because nobody knew how much it was costing me.

Nobody knows how much a 'yes' costs, apart from you.

Nobody knows how much your 'yes' costs, apart from you. Before you agree to something, pause and think of the bigger picture in your diary and resources. Say, 'Let me get back to you', so that you're not tempted to respond off the back of your historic belief that your worth is the sum of what you do. The more I've begun to respect my boundaries, the fewer, less ugly and less lengthy my burnt-out, overwhelmed moments have become. To be able to step off the burnout rollercoaster, it's helpful to do a speedy assessment of the cost of each 'yes', before the word actually escapes your lips. Here are some tips you might find helpful.

Know your load and your limit

The further you drive in a car, the more fuel you need, right? In fact, you need a little extra just in case you have to make a detour, go off-piste to find a toilet, or you get lost. You need to allow for contingency. Once, we set out on the motorway with our fuel tank in the red. The warning light glared at us, yet we were in a rush. So we decided to stop at the first service station to refill en route. The problem was that the service station never appeared, or at least not soon enough. We drove down the slow lane on a wing and a prayer, knowing that every mile we covered was just luck, and soon that luck would run out. The accelerator became spongy and we veered off to the safety of the hard shoulder. After hours of waiting for a tow truck, we climbed aboard the lorry, awkwardly saying to the driver, 'Oh dear, this must happen all the time.' His response, 'Not as much as you think', had us sinking into the plastic seating even further.

So often, this is how I live my life. I hover around the red zone of my resources, winging it. I know I'm low on energy, time and zest for life, yet I keep powering on regardless. This is not a kind way to live. It's not a nice way to live, and it keeps you wedged firmly in your seat of the burnout rollercoaster. You either schedule in fuel stops, or you grind to a messy, inconvenient halt. I like to think that self-respect is all about keeping a healthy contingency space between your load and your limit.

Your load: your load is made up of everything you are responsible for and everything that demands your energy, be it physical, emotional, spiritual or mental. Your load is forever changing depending on how many 'yeses' you dish out and how busy your life is.

Your limit: your limit is the sum of the resources you have available to use. This is also constantly changing. Your resources are impacted by how well you've slept, what support you have, whether you've eaten, how self-nurturing your behaviour is, and what meaningful relationships you've drawn from recently.

Your contingency: your contingency is the extra bit of fuel in your tank. It's your reserve, should you need it. It's the energy you draw upon when one of life's curveballs knocks you, or you catch a cold or are needed for a few extra hours in the office after a busy day. You need this contingency so that these curveballs don't find you utterly floored and empty, scraping from the bottom of an already empty barrel.

If your friend was unwell, would you push them to party? Probably not, because you'd respect that their resources were low. You'd recognise that they were having to use their reserves of energy simply to maintain the doggy paddle of life. In the same way, continually pushing yourself beyond the limits of your energy is not respectful. It's unkind, maybe even cruel sometimes. And what message are you giving yourself? That you are not worthy of rest or recovery? That your human limitations aren't good enough?

You may have become so used to living in the red zone, that it feels alien and awkward for you to refuel. Have you ever felt a wave of guilt when you've stopped, slowed down, booked a holiday, put your out-of-office on, taken a sick day, paused, put your feet up or said no? If so, then you've got used to living at the very limit of your resources. It's time to change things up for the sake of your mental health and self-esteem. You are worthy of rest. You are more than what you do. End of story. (But not the end of the book!)

You are worthy of rest.

Rest as recovery

For years, I stayed up past midnight, getting stuff done, and then I got the flu. It got me into the habit of going to bed earlier, and I couldn't believe it. I always thought I was an irritable person. But I became so much calmer. Rest basically changed my personality. Sure, I don't get as much stuff done, but I'm nicer to be around!

Patty

For so long, I viewed rest as an indulgence. A worthless and unproductive waste of time. And then one day, I started seeing it as a kind of recovery! Rest offers recovery from getting caught up in a fast-paced life, from giving and doing. It's not indulgence; it's science: when we give, we need to replace or we'll end up in debt. Rest is the antidote to burnout. It's the ticket out of overwhelm. You can try to cheat the system with coffee, efficiency, life-hacks and short-cuts. But nothing, *nothing*, replaces rest. When I give without replacing, I become a big old exhausted vacuum. Rest is recovery, or at least you can start to see it as recovery if that helps – until you actually begin to believe you're worthy of rest, regardless of how much or little you've spent of yourself. Because you're also worthy of rest purely for its own sake too! We need rest to give us energy, and we need energy for so much in life.

Do you know what struck me recently? That when I am worn out and overwhelmed, I feel low and I don't laugh as much. Intrusive thoughts come a little thicker and faster, and I find myself overthinking. I just don't have as much joy in my life and start to question whether depression is knocking at my door. And then when I sleep or slow down, the life comes back. This is because we all need that contingency of energy and resources not only to help us navigate the curve-balls, but to be able to enjoy the things that make life good.

You need energy to laugh, because it allows you to push worries aside and just be in the moment. You need energy to bat away intrusive thoughts, rather than let them steamroll over you. You need energy to rationalise overthinking and those irrational, fearful thoughts that threaten to take over and steal your sleep and peace. You need energy to invest in the relationships that are meaningful to you, and to engage in activities that give you purpose or happiness. All of these things require energy. And if you're letting rest become deprioritised and squeezed out of your life like some sort of wasteful inconvenience, a whole lot of other stuff goes out too. How much rest you have has a lot to do with your general sense of wellbeing.

To sum up

The way you treat yourself is an important key to believing that you are worth having your needs met; just as the way you talk to yourself in your thoughts is important too. The two need to work in tandem. Actions say so much, but we also know how powerful the spoken word is. I remember things that were said to me flippantly decades ago, so how much more impact could a drip-fed critical narrative have on my self-esteem? Therefore, address the way you speak to and treat yourself in tandem.

Self-care and self-respect aren't selfish.

Try to be patient with yourself in this process. It's like learning a new language or exercising an unused muscle. It can feel tiring because it requires focus and intention, but in time you'll become stronger at speaking to and treating yourself more respectfully. Self-care and self-respect aren't selfish;

they are a way of nurturing your self-esteem so that you can feel deserving of the good things and relationships in your life, and believe you are worthy of seeking support when you need it.

JOURNAL POINTS

- How would someone feel if you treated them in the way you treated yourself?
- In what ways do you deny yourself self-respect? How do you feel when you do?
- What are your needs now? List three things.
- What is your attitude to rest? How might you get more of it?
- How much contingency do you allow between your load and your limit? How might you change that if necessary?

Chapter 9

Pressing pause on people-pleasing

Mantra: *It is a fact, and not a failing,*
that I cannot please everyone.

I'm going to share a poem I wrote a few years ago. I didn't write it to share with any eyes other than my own, so if you'd have told me I'd be sharing it in a book one day, I would have said, 'No chance!' But the wonderful thing is that the more we work on our self-esteem, the less we fear what others think of us. So I'm sharing this poem in the hope it might empower you as you continue the journey of working on your self-esteem. This poem is all about the fact that we weren't brought into this world purely to meet the needs and feelings of others. Remember, addressing people-pleasing isn't about 'me first'; it's simply 'me too'. I hope that you feel your shoulders unclench and your spine straighten as you read through . . .

Take your space

A string of 'sorry' falling from my lips,
An unconsidered reflex,
For brushing your leg with my bag as I walked by.
A single seat left on the tube,
Tired legs and pregnant bump ignored
By myself but not by others,
Standing resolute;
A teen with a confident swagger collapses into space I
*   didn't claim.*
She knew she was worth it.

Imposter syndrome.
You'll discover I'm not worthy of your cost,
Of time and energy,
So I'll not rudely shatter your momentary illusions,
I'll just sit quietly.
You'll find your own way to my conclusion soon enough.

Swallowed words,
Too many spoken over,
Mown down by a barrage of other people's noise,
Misunderstood,
Leaving me with echoes
Of my own dialogue in my mind.
Louder voices drowning out
Stuttered attempts to verbalise.
Step back and shut down.

It's so much easier to be less,
Than to relentlessly fight for space amongst the more.

Silenced needs –
I'll meet them myself;
Why burden another with my words and wants,
When I can silently scrape together my own resources?
Furious self-sufficiency
Maketh man a lonely island.

Words of others like sticky Post-it notes,
Assumed as truths and ruminated over,
Until they became tattooed onto a heart that couldn't fight
        them as false.
Surely the minority,
Uttering spiky words or causing unintentional pain,
Are better placed to tell me who I am,
To see the bad in my good.
Hey,
I'll let you assign my price.

Accepting gifts with an awkward shuffle and blushing cheeks,
Compliments ricocheting off the heart,
Like pebbles skimmed off a taut sea,
Bending a burdened back backwards,
Spewing saccharine sentences I don't even believe,
So that you like me.
You could write poetry about your like for me;
It won't be enough for me to believe that that's your truth.

You wish you were older,
A little bit taller,
Somewhat quieter,
A lot more wiser,
Much more patient,
Less outrageous,
Lower maintenance,
More contagious.

I need to be more.
I need to be less.

STOP.

No more envying those walking,
Taking space and talking sentences without apology,
Claiming seats without a sorry,
Requesting quenching water without a tensing of the
       shoulders.

No more swallowing words out of fear,
As to whether they will be mistaken or misunderstood,
Which they may,
In fact they will,
But that is not a reflection of the value of them being heard.

You're a messy complexity of humanity,
With needs and wants and sometimes profanity,
Of ugliness and sweat and space and pride and love and need,

And that's okay.
Flex the muscle of your voice,
Throw out your arms and claim your space that was yours
        all along,
Stop ending sentences with questions and prefixing with 'just',
Because
You
Are
Never
'JUST'
Anything.

Exercise the sinews of your voice box,
No speaking in whispers and avoiding confrontation,
Don't devalue your innate worth with apologies and intonations.

Learn to grow to love your powerful voice,
As a lioness recognises the authority of her roar.
The thoughts and feelings of others about you are neither facts
        nor your business,
Just seen through their scratched grey lenses of experiences,
The one you see them through too, mind you,
We all do.

Unshrug those shoulders you don't need,
To shrink into yourself anymore,
Stop chipping away at a body that takes up precious inches,
Because you are of more value than all the space you could
        ever inhabit,

Laugh freely regardless of snorts and tears,
Your joy is worth experiencing,
And each peal of laughter will become easier,
Even if it's only you who understands the joke.

Walk stronger,
Hold your head higher,
Line lips in crimson red and wear colour,
Or don't.
But if you don't,
Don't because you don't want to,
Not because you want to but fear being seen.
Your purpose might feel entangled and confused,
But you have purpose all the same,
That's a promise.

You don't need to be less,
You don't need to be more.

Take your space.
Take your space without apology,
Without bended knee or slipping into the comfort of the
        background,
Grow slowly but surely in to yourself.

You
Are
Never
'JUST'.

So, this is what this chapter is about. The biggest and most obvious external shift that has come with working on my self-esteem has been in the way I relate to others. For most of my life, I felt 'less than', and this came out in pretty much every single interaction I had. My main aim was to please. I felt worthless and worth less than others, so I needed to work extra hard to earn acceptance and approval.

Nurturing self-esteem allows you to enjoy healthier and more balanced relationships. But what does this look like and how do you start to do things differently, if your main priority has been to please others? I'm going to answer that question for you. I'm also going to touch on the unspoken costs of these changes too.

What is people-pleasing?

Whenever I go to people's houses, even just for a cup of tea, I take a gift. My friends tell me not to. I'm in debt, so I shouldn't. But I feel guilty that they are hosting me. It's a way of repaying their kindness.

Anonymous

When I talk about people-pleasing, I'm not just talking about those moments in which you please others; I'm talking about when pleasing others becomes a lifestyle, a purpose or the main way you spend your energy. For many of us people-pleasers, there is a deep fear that comes with dis-pleasing people – so much so, that we'd do almost anything to avoid it. Even if people-pleasing comes at the cost of our own mental health and happiness.

I call myself a people-pleaser in recovery. I will always be 'in recovery'. Like an addict who knows that if they step away from their recovery programme, they will likely fall back into the behaviour from which they've tried so hard to save themselves, I must always monitor this impulse in myself, because it costs too much not to. People-pleasing has cost me a lot. For as long as I can recall, I've believed this to be my sole purpose in life: to please others and keep them happy. For very many years, I neglected and overlooked my needs, feelings and unique character in order to please others. I hoped this could somehow compensate for the fact that, deep down, I believed myself to be unlovable and unworthy.

People-pleasing is when you gain your self-esteem from how others see you.

When I talk about people-pleasing, I'm not speaking from the perspective of someone who has mastered it, but of someone who is constantly coaching herself through it with varying degrees of success, and who always will be. People-pleasing is when you gain your self-esteem from how others see you. It's the calculation that your worth is the sum of what others think. If someone is pleased or happy as a direct result of what you've done, this makes you feel worthy and acceptable. However, if someone is displeased, judgemental, hurt or unhappy with you, the result is the absolute opposite and your self-esteem is sent plummeting.

Looking to pleasing others to boost your self-esteem is like investing all your money – every single penny of it – in an incredibly volatile stock market. One minute, you are quids in, the streets are paved with gold and you have a spring in your step. Yet the next, you're wondering how on earth you're going to pay for a carton of milk.

The warm glow of knowing I've made someone happy is like golden honey inside my body, oozing down from my chest to my feet. But displeasing someone? Suddenly my heart rate rockets, my shoulders tense, and I feel sick and agitated. It's like white noise buzzes in my ears and I can focus on nothing else. (As I type this, it reminds me exactly of how I described the feeling of shame in chapter 6.) How about you?

When you give others the power to tell you who you are – to assign your price – you put your heart in their hands. They could massage it, or throw it against the wall. Displeasing others taps into feelings of shame and a sense of worthlessness. We can learn to gently coach ourselves through those moments.

Know this: you are not the sum of what people think. You are not the sum of how others behave towards you. Neither positively nor negatively. You are more than that which can be defined by the fleeting, changing thought of another.

People-pleasing

I once heard someone describe people-pleasing as 'people-pleading'. It struck me, because I'd always considered my behaviour to come from a place of giving, not needing. I'd seen my people-pleasing as a sort of charitable behaviour, but calling it 'pleading' made it sound kind of ... needy. On further reflection, I realised that of course there is something transactional about people-pleasing. In truth, the reason I was giving myself so freely to others was because I wanted something back from them that meant more to me. I valued their opinion over my own resources.

People-pleasing puts a pressure on the receiver.

People-pleasing puts a pressure on the receiver. For example, say I agree to make a birthday cake for a friend's child, despite the fact we have other commitments over the weekend. I know it will be challenging and that I don't really have time, but I feel compelled to say yes. I then spend hours in the kitchen, stressed and snappy, making cake layers between organising playdates and having to dash out for extra ingredients before the shops shut. I ice the cake late at night through tired eyes. I hand it over to a brief, 'Ah, thank you so much – it's wonderful.' Enter those familiar feelings of resentment and hurt that come when I can't really afford the 'yes' that I've offered.

However, my friend doesn't know the real cost of that cake to me, the hours and energy poured into it. She will have assumed that if I said I could do it, then I must have had the available time and resources to bake it. After all, I am responsible for placing the boundaries around my resources! Me and only me. Yet I needed more thanks and acknowledgment from her than she knew to give. In baking that cake, I was giving more to her than she would have ever been willing to ask for, had she known my diary!

Say I agreed to make the cake because I knew I had the time to do it. It wasn't stressful; in fact, it was enjoyable. I handed it over to a simple 'thank you', and walked off happy. There was no hidden cost. Resentment and hurt sit in the gap between what we give and what we hope to get. When you place boundaries around what you give, what you get in return has less influence on your self-esteem.

Characteristics of people-pleasing

Here are some characteristics of people-pleasing behaviour. See if any of them resonate. There's no need to score yourself – it's not an assessment!

A people-pleaser may be described as . . .

- Thoughtful
- Sensitive
- Empathetic
- Always willing to help
- A good listening ear
- The agony aunt/uncle
- Dependable
- Loyal
- Caring
- Kind
- A peace-keeper

A people-pleaser may experience a drive to . . .

- Put everyone first regardless of the cost
- Apologise profusely, even for things that aren't their fault
- Say 'yes' when they mean 'no'
- Avoid hurting or upsetting others, even if it costs them significantly
- Dissect social interactions to reassure themselves that they haven't upset anyone
- Feel anxiety, stress or shame if they feel misunderstood or believe they've caused upset
- Avoid expressing true feelings, opinions, needs or emotions that may cause conflict or disagreement
- Choose to agree with others, even if they think differently
- Be kinder to others than they are to themselves
- Reject compliments
- Avoid asking anything of others
- Avoid confrontation
- Reject offers of support and generosity
- Display different characteristics depending on who they are with
- Quickly correct anything they may have done wrong
- Defend themselves by pre-empting attack and doing whatever they can to appease people
- Seek compliments, affirmation and reassurance
- Move their own personal boundaries according to the situation

But what's wrong with pleasing others?

You don't need to change shape to please the world.

One of my worries about addressing my drive for people-pleasing was that I'd be transformed into some kind of outspoken, brash bully who demands the world to move aside for them. It's true that there is nothing wrong with pleasing others. The challenge comes when pleasing someone else is driven by your need to gain a sense of approval, validation or acceptance. Or that the thought of displeasing someone finds you feeling invalidated and unacceptable, not just to that individual but as a person. You don't need to change shape to please the world.

The cost of continually denying yourself in order to please others is high. Because the cost is you. You are the cost. Your authentic self becomes the collateral damage – the denied, the neglected and the overridden. For me, pleasing others wasn't so much a choice as an absolute necessity. My self-esteem became so enmeshed in how others felt about me that I had to do all that I could, within my power, to keep those around me happy, comfortable and pleased. If I didn't, who was I?

Today, even though I'm still working on my people-pleasing tendencies, my drive to please others is generally different. It's more of a choice than a necessity. I want to please others because it feels good; because it's kind and it makes life nicer. Sometimes it *does* cost me and it *is* sacrificial, and it means choosing to prioritise the needs of others over my own. However, it's still my choice and my boundaries are in a different place.

Whilst I may put aside my own needs or feelings, I will *not* (or at least I try not to) neglect who I am. Sometimes, in order not to neglect myself, I have to risk displeasing someone by holding my boundaries: I may have to disagree with them or say 'no'; I may have to express my hurt or disappointment; I may have to seek or accept support, knowing that I'm making demands on another person's resources in some way. Working on my internal dialogue and trying to treat myself with kindness and respect are what enable me to navigate these different challenges. For example, if I feel I've displeased someone, where my internal dialogue might once have branded me a failure and unworthy of good friendships, it now tries to restore balance and bring a compassionate perspective.

Choosing how to respond

The ways in which you treat and speak to yourself form the foundation from which you respond to challenges and influence where you place your boundaries in relationships (see chapters 7 and 8 for a refresh on this). If your self-esteem is at a low, you're far more likely to want to please others in order to boost it – even if this is at your own expense. If your self-esteem is in a healthy place, you're more likely to be able to coach yourself through those challenging moments, seeing them for what they are, rather than letting them become statements of who you are.

Here's another example. Say my friend has sent me a text message, asking if we can chat as she's had an argument with her boyfriend. I'm finishing off some work and was about to jump in the shower before meeting my husband for a long-awaited date-night dinner.

People-pleasing feeling: *I have to call her now. She needs me. I don't want her to think I'm not there for her. She might be upset with me.*

People-pleasing behaviour: *I call her immediately as I want to be there for her.*

Cost: *I haphazardly finish my work. I don't have time for the shower I'd been putting off all day. I shove on an outfit that I later realise is dirty. I turn up sweaty, rushed and late for dinner. I feel resentful and irritated at my friend for taking up so much time when I was in a rush for a dinner my husband and I have been trying to diarise for months (even though she has no idea about this!).*

Now for an alternative:

Internal discussion: *I don't have to call her now. She needs me and I can be there for her, but I want to be able to focus properly on what she has to say. I'm in a rush now and have somewhere to be. Now is not the best time, but I can make time.*

Behaviour: *I text her back: 'Oh, love. I'm sorry things are tough. I'm dashing around right now, but I can give you a quick call in the car on the way to dinner. Otherwise we can chat properly on the phone in the morning or meet for coffee at nine once I've dropped the kids off at school. Let me know. Thinking of you, xxx.'*

Cost: *An hour of my time talking through the argument. But she is my friend, I love her and I really want to be there for her. So, sure, it costs my time and attention, but it's a price I am very willing to pay.*

In this situation, putting healthy boundaries around my giving doesn't turn me into a dismissive ogre. I don't end up ignoring my friend's needs. It just means that I pause to look at the bigger picture in this scenario and assess the cost of acting immediately. When you address people-pleasing, your reactions become less fear-driven, and more considered. What's more, you challenge any assumptions or fears about whether good relationships can or cannot withstand healthy boundaries.

> **When you address people-pleasing, your reactions become less fear-driven.**

It might help to know that when you have been living so far at one end of the people-pleasing spectrum, you are incredibly unlikely to swing straight to the other end! Be kind to yourself as you navigate this transition. It takes time; it's about trial and error, and it's a new way of responding to situations. There can be throwbacks and repercussions as you establish new boundaries and start saying 'no' where you may have before said 'sure'.

People-pleasing and perfectionism

I think I managed thirty-one years of being nice to everyone and terrified of getting anything wrong — until I had nothing left in myself to give. Things had to change. I had to exist for more than other people and high standards.

Zeena

If you're a perfectionist and a people-pleaser, then you'll likely be utterly exhausted. The two can be so intertwined. To be a perfectionist in pleasing others is a relentless pursuit. When your self-esteem is based upon how well you do, and how much you please others, you will forever be trying and often feeling disappointed. Hopefully, as you address perfectionism and find the truth in the fact that you are neither the sum of what you do, nor how well you do it, you'll see this positively shift your people-pleasing drive. People-pleasing is about perfectionism applied to relationships.

Noes can be nice!

Sometimes it's awkward to say no, but it's the right thing and I feel my shoulders drop and some stress exit my body. It's like a physical thing for me.

Ali

When you say no, you can do it gently! Consider the fact that not every 'no' has hurt you in the past, or felt like a rejection. When you say no, you are giving yourself the opportunity to respect the other person through not saying yes and then doing something resentfully! Saying no means that you can say yes to other things – such as another opportunity, a clearer diary or simply enjoying a rest.

That said, it's absolutely fine to say yes; just take a moment to question what is driving your reply. Are you saying yes because:

- You feel fearful, e.g. *I'm worried you'll feel rejected and like me less.*
- You feel obligated even though you aren't, e.g. *I don't want to go to the wedding of an acquaintance who bullied me at school, but she asked, so I feel obliged.*
- You need to, because it's required of you, e.g. *I don't really feel like going to work but I must.*
- You choose to spend your energy that way, e.g. *I am tired, but this friend means a lot to me and I choose to spend my energy on this relationship.*

There are so many variables that come with each situation. Sometimes your 'no' might cost you a lot, or genuinely hurt the other person. You may regret it – or feel utterly empowered by it. You may receive push-back (*oh, come on, you did it last time . . .*) or be surprised to find your refusal happily accepted! Today, it might be fine to say yes to something that you would have said no to yesterday! The important thing is that you take yourself into consideration when you reply, rather than completely overlooking

Take yourself into consideration when you respond.

yourself. It's all a learning process! Here are some gentle responses I find helpful:

- 'Let me get back to you. I need to check the diary.'
  (*This gives me a moment to think and means I'm less likely to jump in with a 'yes' when perhaps I mean 'no'.*)
- 'I can't make that day, so what about next week?'
- 'Thank you so much for asking, but I'm all right for the moment.'
- 'I'm tired and need an evening to reset, but would love to do another time.'

The fact of the matter is that, for me, it's so important to continue learning how to assert healthy boundaries and say no. A huge motivator for me in addressing this is that I want my own children to feel comfortable asserting their boundaries too. I hate to imagine my little girl ending up in some of the compromising situations I've found myself in, with my timid 'no' hovering deep in the bottom of my stomach and being fearful of giving it voice in case I offended anyone. I even worried about offending those who were offending me! No, I will continue to work on this, so that my children know that whilst showing kindness and respect to others is key, they deserve to be shown kindness and respect too. And sometimes that means saying 'no'.

Recognising the cost of people-pleasing

I stayed in a relationship for eight years that wasn't right for me because I was worried about hurting him if I broke it off. It all came to a head in a way messier way than if I'd have done it years earlier.

Anonymous

I want you to take a moment to consider the cost that people-pleasing has had for you. I'm talking about the times you've said yes, or gone along with something, when the best and most respectful thing for yourself would have been to assert your boundaries. This is because when we say yes, but we mean no, we are turning away from ourselves. If all of our actions and decisions are statements about our perceived worth, what are you saying to yourself?

I've heard people say, 'Anna would cut off her right arm to help someone else.' You know what? I would have and I did, metaphorically speaking. Many times, I've cut off my metaphorical right arm in order to help, please, appease or ease. Yet what happens to me? I'm left with no right arm, although my right arm is a pretty darned important part of my body! Sure, I might have pleased someone else or avoided a confrontation, but the cost to me is huge. How will I carry washing down the stairs, cuddle my kids, swim? Are you cutting off your right arm for something that, when you think about it, isn't deserving of the cost?

Today, you might say, 'Anna, it would make me so happy if you cut off your right arm for me.' And I'd reply, 'I wish you'd accept something less. A cake, a chat perhaps or a hug? But you want my arm? You're just going to have to be unhappy, then! Your happiness cannot depend on something that costs me so highly! I'm keeping my arm.' Yet if my child's life depended on my right arm, sure, take it. It's worth the cost. Sometimes my 'arm' is my time, my energy, my finances, my mental health, my diary space, my rest, my headspace. Sometimes my energy is particularly expensive, because I don't have much of it. Like fuel at the pump, the price goes up with the demand.

Be aware of paying far too high a price through people-pleasing.

Be wary of paying far too high a price through people-pleasing. Saying no to an event might cost you awkwardness, disappointment, a change in friendship dynamic or irritation. Yet it might also gain you self-respect, self-esteem, an opportunity to rest, more headspace and energy to put back into the things that matter most. It's better to be rejected for demanding respect, than to be accepted whilst rejecting yourself.

The benefits of having your noes and your boundaries in better places

I was the person everyone would come to for favours, because I'd never say no. I was scared friends would think I didn't care about them. But I just ended up feeling used and a bit hurt. So, I started to say no when I couldn't, and yes when I was happy to. It's like I never saw 'no' or 'I can't this time' as an option!

Zo

When your boundaries are a little firmer, and your 'no, thank yous' become a little easier, then your life changes too. It becomes more sustainable as you hop off the overwhelm rollercoaster. You have more energy to live, love and laugh! Have you ever felt too tired to laugh? By addressing people-pleasing, you are literally giving yourself the gift of enjoying the good things in your life more often. And you are giving those who care about you more of a chance to enjoy you too! My family enjoy me so much more when my boundaries and my noes are in the right places. I am less irritable, stressed, burnt out and exhausted. I owe it to myself, I owe it to them.

When you say 'yes', when a 'no, thank you' would be most beneficial, you can feel frustrated, resentful, self-critical, used or disempowered. These feelings can drive your self-esteem down. When you put a healthy boundary in place, whilst sometimes it can seem hard and make things tricky to navigate, you can end up feeling empowered, self-respecting, preserved and energised. What's more, your self-esteem enjoys a boost because you have acknowledged and respected your thoughts, needs and feelings.

Giving, sacrificing and spending your resources can become a conscious choice instead of a consistent fear-driven, knee-jerk reaction. Life and people will *always* want something from you, but you have finite resources. We need to stop living as if our resources are infinite, because it is expensive to live this way. It costs a lot to give what you haven't got to give. It costs you. And you're worth far more than spending all your resources on pleasing others. You deserve to be pleased and supported too!

Someone doesn't like you

I can't stand the thought of someone thinking something bad about me.

Keira

You know what? I felt guilty even typing 'someone doesn't like you'! I'm sure you are the loveliest of people, and that I would really enjoy sitting on the sofa and chatting over a cuppa with you. That, I do not doubt for a single second. And I hate thinking that anyone might not like me, yet it's something I am having to consistently, over and over again, come to terms with.

I expressed a dislike for green tea on social media once, and I was hit with a barrage of green-tea lovers suggesting ways I might enjoy it: *try it with lemon, try it iced, add honey, leave the teabag in longer* ... The thing is, no offence to the leafy beverage, but it's just not my cup of tea (pardon the pun). Now, because I don't like green tea, does it mean that green tea is inherently bad? Should it be removed from all the shelves because Anna Mathur in Surrey, England isn't a fan? No, because many people like green tea! Just because I'm not a fan isn't a statement about whether it deserves to be on the shelf. I'm not that special.

Yet, why then, if we know we are not someone's cup of tea, do we take it as a statement of truth? Are they really that special that they get a right to say whether we are good people or not? Worthy or not? Acceptable or not?

One frame of a film

When my mum challenges me, I listen. She knows and loves me better than anyone, even if it hurts a bit to hear.

Angharad

Now, if you're like me, and the thought of someone not liking you feels a bitter pill to swallow, or makes you shuffle in your chair as you think of some way to try to win them over, I want to share a lightbulb moment I had a few weeks ago. It has been a game-changer for me.

Imagine if I were to discourage you from watching a film as your finger hovered over the remote to press play. 'Oh gosh,' I say. 'Don't watch that one. The plot's weak, the main actor doesn't say a thing and there's absolutely no chemistry between the couple.' Would your finger waver on the play button? Perhaps you'd skip that film and continue the hunt for your evening viewing. Then, imagine if you discovered I'd only actually caught five seconds of the whole movie. My entire review is based on less than a scene of the whole shebang. What would that do to the trustworthiness of my review? It would make it meaningless! How can I so confidently review a film I haven't even watched? You'd probably decide, in that case, that you quite like the look of it and you'll give it a shot! Fair enough!

We often place so much value on the feedback of those who only glimpse mere moments of our entire lives. I have felt the judgemental glances of fellow supermarket shoppers when one of my kids has had a tantrum over not getting a gingerbread man. Sure, they may judge, but they don't know the full story of my morning, or my son. So their judgement only really has the same amount of value as my rubbish film review! Goodness me, I've given away one hell of a lot of power in my lifetime. Empowering people who don't even know me to tell me what I am worth.

Now, I'll tell you whose feedback I do value. And that's the feedback of those people in my life who have viewed more than just a single scene. I value the feedback of those individuals who've taken time to understand the plot, and who've sat through the boring credits when most people would have switched off. These are the people who know me, know my story, my heart and my intentions; who are more experienced than me and who want the best for me. They are the people who can frame their feedback or criticism in a kind and considerate way, because they share it with the aim of helping me grow, rather than hurting me.

But do you know what also hit me as I explored this scenario? Whilst it really helped me reframe how I digested criticism or feedback, it also helped me reframe how I value compliments or praise. As someone who has sought compliments and praise as a means of temporarily increasing my self-esteem, this realisation came at me like a rocket: if I am going to believe that the feedback or judgement of those who have only ever seen a single scene or screenshot of my life matters less than I thought, then I must also believe that the compliments or praise of those who have only seen a single scene matter less too.

Because the fact of the matter is, nobody else's feedback makes you worth more or less than you already are. Words shared by the right people can be helpful, insightful, supportive, encouraging, affirming and challenging – but they do not make you worth more.

The unspoken costs of change

I mustered up the courage and told my boss I couldn't do so much unpaid overtime any more. I was tired and had no social life. My worst fear came true – he fired me. Now I work in a different job. I've got my life back.

Anonymous

Imagine watching a sped-up video of a growing oak tree. As it grows from a sapling into a strong, sturdy oak, you watch it gain height and leaves. Yet what you don't see is how the roots disrupt the soil below. They reach out, dig down and spread to accommodate the growth that is seen above the grass. You watch some nearby plants shrivel up as the roots spread beneath them. A nearby bush wilts as the wider canopy of leaves casts a shadow over it. In some places the earth is slowly pushed up, causing mounds and revealing hints of strong, tangled root. Yet the birds come and build their nests in its branches and the squirrels use the trunk as a playground. People come to picnic underneath it, finding respite from the hot sun in the cool shade. In spring, daffodils pop up in a circle around the trunk, happy in the fertile earth and protected from harsh elements.

Growth changes things. Your growth and, with it, your increased understanding of your worth, your stronger noes and moved goalposts and boundaries, will all change things.

You'll see growth and balance where before you felt stuck or depleted. Yet growth isn't all happy squirrels and picnics. Sometimes it's ugly; sometimes certain elements don't last the journey. Moving boundaries changes relationship dynamics. I've seen clients grow in the most incredible ways. But there are sometimes side-effects that aren't so comfortable. As people have begun to thrive in who they are, I've seen lovers break up, friendships drift, and resignations handed in. I've seen conflict and hurt, resentment and confusion.

When we start to say, 'You know what? It's actually not okay for you to treat me like that', or 'Perhaps I am worthy of applying for that job after all', things change. They can't not. Sometimes there is grief to be grieved. But often it's a healthy grief. What has ended, or changed, has changed in a good way – albeit uncomfortable or painful. Perhaps it had been causing some kind of pain for a long time.

When I began to set limits and boundaries, some people found this challenging to accept. Generally, these were the people who had benefited most from my lack of boundaries. I can imagine that it must feel inconvenient when the person who you used to depend on to always say yes, begins to say no sometimes. In one job, I was always the first to volunteer to run additional errands. I wanted to please my colleague. However, the more 'I'll do it's' I offered, the more my work load stacked up as I spent time away from the computer. Stress and resentment simmered under the surface as I spent evenings catching up at home. So, I began to say 'I can't today' when running an errand would jeopardise an evening with a friend, or find me behind in my work. I was met with irritation as people had to look further afield, but as everyone got used to the fact I didn't always jump up with a 'I'll do it', this new boundary was solidified.

Givers need to set limits, because takers rarely do.

Givers need to set limits, because takers rarely do. It's often not even intentional when people take advantage of people-pleasers! Surely we're all far more likely to ask of those who have a habit of saying yes than those who don't. We generally assume people say yes because they are happy to do what's being asked. We don't see the bigger picture, which includes their packed diary or depleted energy levels; we don't know whether their yes is fuelled by fear or willingness. Therefore we must all learn to take responsibility for our own yeses.

Sometimes you may have to set boundaries that other people don't understand. Because they can't, or don't have the insight, understanding, or capacity to. Sometimes your boundaries can impact wider friendship groups and families. The ripple effects can travel far and wide.

To sum up

I did everything to make Mum happy. I did everything she wanted. Lived at home, ate with her every day. I decided to take the job in France. Five years later, she's still angry. I've had to accept that our relationship will never be the same again. I had to live for more than just her happiness.

Anonymous

People-pleasing is not an easy topic to write about in a single chapter; it deserves a whole book. People-pleasing and boundary-setting can be complicated, with no clear sets of rules to follow. As you learn to value your own responses and grow in confidence when setting your boundaries, you'll become more aware of the choices available to you in different circumstances. It's all about awareness, really: the more aware you become of what you want, need and feel – and the more you come to terms with the fact that you can't please everyone – the more you'll find yourself respecting your boundaries and inviting others to do the same.

I really encourage you to seek support with this issue if you feel it would be beneficial (see Helpful Contacts, page 265). Whether it be a trusted friend or therapist, you deserve to have guidance, insight and support if you wish to address experiences and feelings that may have far-reaching, complicated or painful implications. No healthy form of love, friendship, job or circumstance would ever require you to live in constant denial of who you are. You are worthy of respect, both from yourself and from others. Healthy love does not require you to give yourself away.

JOURNAL POINTS

- How do you feel when you know you've pleased someone?
- How do you feel when you know you've displeased someone?
- How has your need to please others impacted you?
- Consider when you've acted to please others recently. What might you like to do differently if the opportunity arises again?
- Which of your relationships might be challenged if you were to assert healthier boundaries in them? What support do you have available to help you navigate this?

Chapter 10

Claiming confidence

Mantra: I'm in my own lane.

Once I began to address my need to please others, my self-esteem began to slowly creep its way up from its dusty corner on the floor. And as my self-esteem increased, I began to accept myself more for who I was, rather than constantly trying to change myself like a chameleon into who I assumed others wanted me to be. One brilliant side-effect was that my confidence changed too.

Work on your self-esteem – and confidence will follow.

My hope for you is that your confidence will come as you start to set healthier boundaries and assert your voice. I'm not going to give you seven steps on 'how to be confident' in this chapter; instead, we're going to delve into what confidence actually means, and how it's something you don't need to 'make' happen by following steps and tips. Instead, let's imagine a plant. The roots represent the groundwork you have been doing on the subject of worth. The stem is growing tall as you amend the behaviours and habits of decades, enabling the roots to grow stronger in turn to support it. And the flower? Well, that just comes as part of the process. You can't make it bloom, and it can't bloom without good roots. You care for the roots and the flower will take care of itself. You work on your self-esteem – and confidence will follow.

What does confidence mean to you?

I am so jealous of confident people. I want to be like them but I have no idea how.

Anonymous

I've often envied confidence. I've envied those who seem to have an effortless acceptance of who they are. What's more, their apparent lack of need for other people's acceptance somehow invites even more acceptance from others. I've sometimes felt intimidated in the presence of a confident person, because their confidence only served to emphasise to me how much confidence I lacked. However, around some confident people, I'd find myself temporarily growing in confidence; for if they seemed unfazed by having a different opinion to others, or by asking for something they need (such as a glass of water or a seat), maybe they didn't need me to agree with everything they said? And maybe I could express a need to them in return? Sometimes, being around people who seemed unfazed by being true to themselves can gave me the liberty to be myself too.

I tried to be confident when I was younger. I faked it.

I remember being aged thirteen at secondary school when one of the 'popular' girls told me that if I wanted to be popular and liked, I simply needed to put on a happy voice, smile lots and call everyone 'honey' whilst touching them on the arm. I am not making this up! I tried her tips and just felt awkward, like I was being fake. I can't quite remember whether it worked. I'd look at those around me and try to emulate their mannerisms as if I could somehow morph myself into being a more popular person by attempting to be like them.

Confident people seem to be more liked, happier and more successful. But above all, the most attractive and desirable thing about them for me, was that they just seem to be comfortable being themselves. And as someone who experienced a constant, squirming sense of there being something wrong with me, or something fundamentally unlovable, I wanted that. I wanted to feel that confidence so badly. Perhaps then people might accept me. And if they accepted me, maybe I could accept me. Spoiler alert: it took me years and years to realise it doesn't work that way. Acceptance comes when you come to terms with the fact that you'll never be entirely acceptable to others. Therefore making it my life-long aim – to ensure everyone was pleased with me – did nothing but take my self-esteem on that roll-ercoaster of buzzing highs and self-doubting lows.

The confidence con

I dieted for three decades, believing that if I hit my goal weight, I'd finally walk into a room without worrying what people think. I felt hot in my wedding dress, but I still didn't feel deserving of the man at the end of the aisle.

Fern

The issue with my old understanding of confidence was that:

1. I believed I needed to be confident in order to be accepted.
2. I needed to be accepted, in order to be confident.

It was a bit of a chicken-and-egg situation, really. And it became trickier when love and acceptance didn't always come from those I desired it from most, in the constantly roaring tidal wave I required to make myself feel confident. When your confidence takes a dive, your self-esteem tends to take a dive too. You can find yourself feeling unworthy of the very things that you look to in order to give you confidence. So even when these things do happen (such as being liked or loved, and other good things happening to you), you may feel suspicious and unaccepting of them.

Sometimes the reason we lack confidence is because we are tempted to compare ourselves constantly to confident individuals. It can be easy to fixate on the 'things' they have or the characteristics they display, assuming that these must be the reason for their confidence. I know I've analysed the relationships, the weight, the jobs of others, assuming these must be the magical factors that give them the kind of confidence that I admire. Then we may commit ourselves to going after those things for ourselves, in the hope that we will gain confidence too. Maybe if we have what they have, we will possess the confidence they have?

But that's a flawed assumption, and cognitively you know it too, I'm sure. There are so many people who, by the world's standards, have 'everything', yet who lack confidence or admit to low self-esteem. I guess they also probably hoped that they'd find confidence at the end of the red carpet, or on the rich list. With the dashing of high hopes comes lashings of disappointment.

Just as people can only see and judge a snapshot of our own lives, it's helpful to recognise where we might be doing the same to others. When we realise that we've taken a snapshot of someone else's life and idealised it, or expanded it into our imagined version of the fuller picture, we can remind ourselves that all is not as we perceive it to be; meaning we're less likely to use these faulty perceptions as a basis for comparison. The thing is, like me, you've probably spent so much time and energy looking for confidence in places where it cannot be found. Just as with self-esteem, when you seek confidence from things outside yourself, you will always be left wanting more.

Confidence isn't gleaned purely from hitting goals (although our economy sure thrives on us believing that to be true), but is based upon your perception of yourself. Therefore, improving certain aspects of your life will never truly have the power to straighten your spine or relax your shoulders and make you stand tall as you enter a room.

Confidence is a state of mind: the feeling that you accept yourself regardless of how you compare to others.

What is confidence?

Confidence isn't something that can just be 'fixed'. I find it such a relief to know that some things simply aren't fixable. It provides me with hope that things can organically change for the better. Confidence isn't about being extrovert, loud or having a big presence. We know that those qualities may actually come from low self-esteem. Instead, here's a brief summary of what an extrovert and an introvert are:

Extrovert: *you'd rather be around others than spend time alone. Being sociable energises you, and spending quality time with people fills you up!*

Introvert: *you prefer to spend quality time with smaller groups than larger ones. You benefit from having the time to process your thoughts and feelings. When you've been busy or sociable, you find it helpful to retreat to recharge.*

As with everything, you can fall somewhere between the two! I quite like the term 'ambivert', which describes someone who has a balance of extrovert and introvert features, and which reminds me that it's quite normal to swing between two poles! While there's no need to label yourself, thinking about these personality types can help you recognise where you might be idealising someone else's personality traits.

When I reach my social or busyness limit, it can feel quite physical! My stress response kicks in and I need to get some space. In my university days, my friends would laugh because I'd often be partying on the dancefloor and then suddenly disappear. They'd text me to find my whereabouts and I'd be in bed! I used to feel so frustrated, like a failure when I needed to retreat while others seemed quite happy to continue socialising. But the more I've respected this trait in myself, the more I have prioritised my own space.

Confidence does not look the same for everyone.

As I've removed the pressure for me to be different to who I am, or feel differently to how I feel, I have started to accommodate my need for space where I can, and no longer shame myself for it. I try not to fill my diary to the same extent, or push myself to remain at social events until everyone leaves. As I've tweaked my boundaries to accommodate my needs more, that 'get me out of here *now*' stress response doesn't rise up as often. The more you understand yourself, the more you can respect yourself for the way you are wired. Someone can be confident and an introvert. Just as you could be an extrovert who lacks confidence! Confidence does not look the same for everyone.

I have a 'quiet' friend, who is confident. I remember meeting her about fifteen years ago and assuming that she must be shy, because she seemed more of an observer than the life and soul of the party. It didn't take me long to realise that she just didn't feel a need to be loud to fit in with other people's idea of confidence. When she had something to say, she said it. When she had a need, she expressed it. In her quietness, she was simply being authentic and true to herself; neither adding nor taking away from herself in order to appease or please others.

Confidence is self-acceptance

Confidence is self-acceptance. It's not saying:

- I'll never change.
- I'm perfect.
- I love myself *exactly* as I am.

It is saying:

- I accept myself as I am in this moment, even in those areas where I am lacking.
- I accept myself as I change and work on things.
- I accept myself as I grow, not only when I have grown or changed, or gained, or lost, or moved, or got that promotion.

Is acceptance of yourself really acceptance if it comes with conditions? Can you really accept yourself when you are rejecting those parts of yourself that haven't met your own standard yet? Confidence should not be a goal-orientated exercise. If it comes with a 'when', be warned – it's not true self-acceptance. *I will accept myself* when *I weigh less. I will accept myself* when *I have the job, the house, the partner,* then *I will feel confident* . . . No, confidence is a call to accept yourself during the journey. It's an acknowledgement that you grow as you go.

We wouldn't say to a toddler, 'I'll only accept you when you walk.' If we did, the pressure for them to walk in order to gain acceptance would scupper their learning process. They would be afraid of being told off when their little legs stumble. Similarly, if you were to tell yourself, 'I'll accept myself *when* I get the promotion', the self-criticism that comes as you stumble towards your goal will negatively impact your self-esteem and confidence. We can end up sabotaging and stifling ourselves when we approach things like this. What if you were to get the promotion that your confidence was so hooked upon, only to discover your colleague had been promoted above you? Then what? Does the goal have to move again? And what if you are made redundant? Then what? Your confidence will dip and dive with the circumstances – unless you detach it from them. It's nice to do well, but it doesn't change your self-worth.

Confidence is the belief that you have the ability and resources to cope with challenges; and it is also the acceptance that if you don't, then you're worthy of support and help – and you will seek this and welcome it. Confidence isn't the lack of acknowledgement of shortcomings, imperfections, failures, dark corners and messy bits; it's the acceptance and choice to respect yourself in full awareness of them and as you work on them. Confidence doesn't require an inflated understanding of who you are, but relies on a realistic one.

- Confidence says: *I might have failed, but I am not a failure.*
- Confidence says: *I can do this, but I don't have the ability to do that. Can you help me?*
- Confidence says: *I accept that I am human!*
- Confidence says: *He doesn't like me, but that's okay. I don't like everyone equally either.*
- Confidence says: *Just because not everyone laughs at my joke doesn't mean it's not worth telling.*
- Confidence says: *I haven't got there yet but I'm trying and I'm on my way . . .*

The fear

When I started to try and accept myself, warts and all, it felt like the pressure had lifted. Things feel better without the fear of getting it wrong all the time.

Anonymous

Surely, if I become accepting of my own failures, I may be more likely to actually become a failure? Maybe if I accept my flaws, I might stop caring about those parts of myself that would actually benefit from change? Personally, I don't think so. Self-acceptance means you are less likely to heap a ton of criticism, judgement and sabotage upon yourself when you stumble on the journey. Which you will do. Because you are human. You'll be less likely to attach your self-esteem, sense of purpose and meaning to goals that offer a rush of self-acceptance which then disappears on the breeze.

Why do I struggle with confidence?

Knowing people were happy with me gave me a boost of confidence.
But I always felt a bit suspicious of people who were nice to me.

Amy

Confidence improves when you come to terms with the fact that your worth is fixed and immovable. I know we explored the causes of low self-esteem in chapter 6, but as a reminder, they can include your cultural background, trauma, how you've been treated, and how you were parented. Low confidence comes down to lack of belief in your worth. You are likely struggle with confidence when you believe that your most authentic self is neither good enough nor deserving of good things. You believe that you need to contort yourself into constantly being something or someone else – to be somehow more or less than who you actually are – in order to be accepted. You believe that confidence comes from being accepted by others, when really it can only come from being accepted by yourself.

Confidence can only come from being accepted by yourself.

Confidence and self-esteem, in my understanding, are intertwined like tree roots that grow twirling and tangling together. If you struggle with self-esteem, you inadvertently struggle with true confidence. I say 'true confidence' because false confidence isn't true confidence; it's an act. And a tiring one at that.

Social anxiety

I am no longer terrified to walk into the office. That has changed my life.

Anonymous

We cannot talk about confidence without touching on social anxiety. Often, the fear around what others think of us can impact our ability to enjoy social situations. This form of anxiety can show itself physical and mentally, even if it's not immediately apparent to others.

I had learnt how to appear confident by studying others and replicating their behaviour. I'd talk confidently and warmly, smiling and asking questions. I tended to be in people-facing jobs. If you had watched me, you'd have thought I was confident. In fact, you probably wouldn't have questioned it. But here's the truth, here's what you didn't see: internally, my mind was running at 100mph. I felt physically awkward, especially if I was standing up and chatting.

My worst nightmare was a networking event that meant standing around and talking to numerous people. It was like I didn't quite know where to put my own hands. I'd become hypersensitive to both my body and interactions with others. I'd worry about the pauses between sentences, and I'd be lining up questions to ask before people had even answered my current one. I'd worry intensely about coming across as being too much, boring, awkward, overbearing or underwhelming. *Am I talking too much? Or not enough? Do I seem interested enough?* At times, I'd feel a physical sense of panic. My fight-or-flight stress response would kick in;

I'd feel sick, sweaty and have this overwhelming urge to escape. I'd look for the exit and every fibre of my being wanted to flee.

Regardless of whether I stayed, or made an excuse and a speedy exit, that wouldn't be the end of the matter. I'd then replay many of the conversations over and again, scrutinising them for hints that I might have unintentionally upset or annoyed someone. Did they like me? Did they secretly think I was stupid? I feared people thinking negatively of me in some way. And that would potentially have a major cost, because it only affirmed the fact that I'd never be accepted, even when I was trying so hard.

It was absolutely exhausting. But as I addressed self-worth and began to coach myself through those moments, things changed. I'd breathe away the feeling of heightened adrenalin and anxiety in toilet cubicles. Inhaling for four counts, exhaling for six. I'd interrupt my overthinking by counting back from one hundred in threes. I became increasingly aware of the assumptions I was making and the fears that lay behind them.

Another important lightbulb moment for me was the realisation that I was taking responsibility for the smoothness of every conversation. If there was a silence, I stepped in. If there was a pause, I asked a question. I took sole responsibility for ensuring that the conversation was what I believed to be a 'good' one. No wonder it was so tiring and anxiety provoking! What a pressure to place on yourself! Conversation occurs between two or more people; it's never fully your sole responsibility. You cannot control the mood, thoughts, opinions, assumptions or conversational skills of other people. If there are awkward silences, misunderstood jokes or miscommunications, that is the very nature of human conversation. We are clunky sometimes; our attention wavers; we get distracted. We will never be two perfect people having a perfect conversation. The more accepting I became of that fact, the less pressure I placed upon myself to take responsibility for things that, quite frankly, weren't my full responsibility at all.

As my self-esteem increased, so did my confidence. Don't get me wrong. It still wavers. I recently went to a press event and experienced that familiar wave of social anxiety. I felt downhearted, but managed to curtail the usual sleep-stealing rumination that would follow. Growth isn't linear. Social anxiety, to me, acts as a small red flag that my self-esteem may have dipped, or that I haven't been making enough space in which to refuel.

I could fill the remainder of this book with tips for coping with social anxiety, but for now, my one tip would be this: work on building healthy self-esteem and reduced social anxiety will be a glorious side-effect. See your social anxiety as a symptom of challenged self-esteem, rather than as a completely separate issue that you have to tackle. However, if you would benefit from some encouragement along the way, please do seek the support of a trusted friend or therapist. (See Helpful Contacts, page 265.)

Physical confidence

*I challenged myself to go outside without my makeup on for the
first time in fifteen years. I felt naked, but the worst anyone said
was, 'Oh, you look tired.' Well, I couldn't take offence at that,
because I was tired.*

Pip

We have it sold to us that there is an ideal body type, shape
and age. Yet it's a fact that people of all shapes and sizes can
be confident, because when your confidence isn't dependent
on how you look but on how you relate to yourself, looks
are no longer the be-all and end-all. Your body and looks
will change over the years regardless of how much cream
is applied to them. If you fixate on a fixed body type and
look, your confidence will waver as these change through
the years.

I remember a time when I'd never leave the house without makeup. Secondary school lunchtimes were spent with
my friends, reapplying concealer in the toilets. When I was
older, I wouldn't let my partner touch my full stomach after
I'd eaten. Now, I'm not saying these things no longer matter
to me, because self-acceptance is a bumpy old road. I still
like to look nice, but I no longer deem myself a lesser being
when I get a bout of hormonal acne, or spy a new grey hair.
I no longer fear what others think about me when I do the
school run in loungewear and no makeup. The following
statements may sound a little cheesy, but sometimes I need
to remind myself of the truth in them:

- You are not worth less because you aren't at your 'ideal weight'.
- You do not deserve to take less space in the world because hormonal spots dot your chin.
- The laughter lines around your eyes don't mean your voice shouldn't be heard.
- Lengthen your spine, drop your shoulders and de-slouch!
- Take up your space.
- How you look is actually the very least interesting thing about you.

If you find this approach challenging, consider what your fears are. Is it the fear of judgement from others? Perhaps you fear your own internal chatter of self-judgement and criticism? Is it the fear of people looking at you if you were to share your stripped-back self with them? How might you challenge your attitude gently and confirm to yourself that these are simply fears and assumptions, and not truths?

The more I encourage and nudge myself outside of my comfort zone, the more I realise that perhaps my harshest judge is myself. Instead of focusing on how I present myself visually to the world, I began focusing on how I was treating my body. I started exercising in a way that felt more respectful and kinder to myself than the constant, relentless pounding of a treadmill. I began to drink more water, and to feed myself with food that would sustain me, rather than snacks to silence the hunger pangs. When I notice my self-esteem reattach itself to how I look, I question how I've been treating myself and my body. Because often when I've fallen into treating my body as something that I own rather than something I am, my attitude slips back.

The truth is that I don't 'have' a body; I *am* a body. I can read books and spend hours nurturing my mind, but if I am disrespecting my body, I am not accepting my whole self. How you treat your body is important. It is not a commodity, it is *you*. If you're challenging yourself to start treating yourself with respect and acceptance, it's important that you don't separate your mind from your body.

The truth is that I don't 'have' a body; I am a body.

You are in a different lane

I had this friend who I basically idolised for years and I constantly compared myself to her. She did something I was utterly shocked by. Suddenly I realised how human she was and how I shouldn't have been so harsh on myself.

Anonymous

Whenever you feel tempted to compare your levels of confidence with those of other people, remember that you are running in a different lane. You don't know what costs and resources other people have; you don't see all of their weaknesses or strengths. Sometimes, the most important factors behind confidence are the ones we don't see. It's easy to idealise what we see in others, and then assume that just because they seem to be thriving, this must be indicative of their entire lives. You can copy-and-paste that assumption across their whole existence and conclude that you are failing in comparison.

Many times, I've had people compliment my ability to juggle so much. I can seemingly hold 1,389 different balls in the air whilst herding three kids through town and running errands. Sure, that's the truth in that moment. However, what people don't see of me is the burnout. The times I melt into an emotional heap at home because I've spent every last piece of myself. It's the moment a text message comes through from an old friend and my response is, 'What do they want from me?' because even kind human interaction feels too much. It's the snapping at my husband because I don't want to talk about weekend logistics when I can't muster the energy to think beyond the moment. Everything has a cost. Everything.

We are all running in different lanes. Comparing your journey to someone else's is like comparing a horse to a bird and berating it for not being able to fly. For me, this journey requires regular inner pep talks whenever I find myself idealising the lives or characteristics of others. The more you come to terms with the fact that everyone is very different and their opinions are very subjective, the less you will try to be what you think they want. If you knew how much of the behaviour and opinions of others is shaped by their history, experience and other factors that are beyond your control – and which have absolutely nothing to do with you or how nice you are – you'd give less power and meaning to them.

When you try to be what you think others want, you overlook what you already are. This is something to keep monitoring. Notice where you are pressuring yourself to be in a different place or moving at a different speed. We drive our self-esteem down when we berate ourselves for not being where or who we believe we should be. You are who you are, and you are where you are. Sure, tweak things and find ways to be accountable to others; find ways to be proactive in your growth and change. But bullying and criticising yourself will likely increase a sense of self-esteem – damning shame.

Confidence is a risky business

When I started my current job, I always said I didn't want tea when someone asked. One day I challenged myself to accept the cup of tea. It felt alien, but now if I want one, I'll say yes.

Laura

While comfort zones are comfortable, growth doesn't happen there.

Growing in confidence requires risk. It's risky stepping outside of your comfort zone, because your comfort zone is comfortable for a reason. It may be that you are less likely to face failure, rejection or criticism if you stay there. It's protective, right? If we don't put ourselves in a social situation, we are less likely to say something that will be misunderstood. But while comfort zones are comfortable, growth doesn't happen there. When you try to protect yourself from what you consider bad or uncomfortable, you are also protecting yourself from what could be brilliant, affirming and life-changing.

Say I choose to risk being misunderstood when I speak in front of a crowd? Say I risk being laughed at should I stumble up the steps to the stage, or utter a sentence that comes out tangled up and awkward? What if all of those things were to happen – yet my words helped others? What if I walked away and my heart was full, even if I did cringe at the memory of tripping over my own dress? Every opportunity for growth and affirmation requires risk. Living a full life requires taking risks at every turn. But perhaps the biggest risk of all is what you stand to lose out on if you don't take those risks.

But the more you work on self-esteem, the less those risks hold power – even when the worst does happen. Sure, I fail, but I am not a failure. Sure, that person may laugh at me, but others value my words. Sure, I may stumble, but I can get up again. I may be misunderstood, but many people do understand me. I may feel hurt, but I am worthy of placing healthy boundaries that require respect. Note the things you are not saying about your fears, and gently challenge yourself to express them. In doing so, you will very likely realise that even if your fears were to come to fruition, it would not be so bad. You can learn to encourage yourself through failure, disappointment and embarrassment.

Turn opportunities to take risks into experiments to either prove or disprove your assumptions about what might happen. Once, I challenged myself to ask people to move down a packed London tube to allow a little more breathing space for those standing in the doorway. I had always envied others who, on my busy commute, could request such a thing! I reminded myself that I was as worthy of space as anyone else. Heart racing, I heard the words escape my lips: 'Can you move down, please?' My heart pounded so loudly I was sure people could hear it. Anyway, people shuffled into the spaces in the aisles and those of us who had felt like packed sardines could breathe again. The world didn't stop because of my request. At worst, I was probably met with an eye-roll and vibes mixed with envy or irritation. Just because I may have annoyed someone doesn't mean that in and of myself, I am annoying. We are all a bit annoying sometimes, fact.

That's just a little example, but you'll start to notice where those opportunities arise. Don't beat yourself up for not taking them! Maybe you will next time, maybe you won't. But the important thing is that as you work on your self-esteem, the risks become less relevant because you are less likely to interpret the outcomes as statements of who you are.

A few words on rejection

My mates encouraged me to download dating apps but I was so scared of people swiping by, that I resisted. On my thirty-fifth birthday, I gave in. I found the rejection tough. But then I met my partner, and it made it all worthwhile.

Anonymous

One of the hardest things to tackle has to be the threat of being rejected. Rejection hurts; it feels personal. For me, it's like a physical and emotional curveball knocks my self-esteem; it taps directly into the part of me that doesn't feel good enough. When I feel rejected, I notice that sense of shame come over me. A fear of rejection is the reason why I've pulled away from budding relationships, or avoided putting myself forward for a particular job. I wonder how different my life might have looked if the fear of rejection had had less power over me.

When I feel or face feeling rejected, I find it very powerful to remind myself that it's not me who is being rejected, but just a small part of the entirety of who I am. I am so much more than the part that someone else has decided they don't like, want or agree with. Rejection is absolutely not a statement of my worth, but a statement about the other person's incompatibility with a part of me, or the incompatibility of their opinion of me.

Everything comes with a risk of rejection. We are rejected all the time, sometimes in small ways that don't bother us that much, from unanswered emails and text messages, to a noncommittal response to an invitation. From not being picked first for a team in the playground, to being turned down for a job. Nobody in the world is immune from rejection, yet why can it feel so painful? The most painful rejections tend to come from those who are most important to us, or through situations we've longed for and invested in that haven't worked out. The more you want the relationship to work, the more you want the job or the friendship, the more painful the rejection feels.

Fear of rejection impacts our confidence because it can leave us feeling worthless. I often thought that if I were to avoid all risk, I'd feel safer. However, I realised that not taking risks entails the greatest risk of all: the risk of not living a fulfilling life. If you are forever taking steps to protect yourself from rejection, you will miss out on some wonderfully life-enriching opportunities, experiences and relationships. Like love. Love makes me feel incredibly vulnerable because it puts me at risk of loss and heartbreak; however, it is also the thing that makes my life so good.

Love and loss are two sides of the same coin. We cannot expose ourselves to the good things in life, such as love and relationships, without exposing ourselves to risk in some way.

- Love and loss
- Acceptance and rejection
- Relationship and vulnerability
- Success and failure

You are worthy of love, acceptance, relationships and success. And you are also worthy of finding ways to be supported through the loss, rejection, vulnerability and failure that these might entail. The more you invest in working on your healthy self-esteem, the less you will fear rejection. In fact, be ready for it. I don't mean in the sense of entering a room and being ready to defend yourself, but just an awareness that you may be rejected somehow – and that is not a statement of how valid you are. Remind yourself that not everyone will understand or like you, but many people will; therefore neither their likes nor dislikes are definitive statements about your ability to be understood or liked.

Talk to others about their experiences of rejection and how they overcame it. Read biographies and find inspiration in stories of rejection that paved the way for wonderful opportunities. Some of the most painful rejections in my life have led me through very fertile territory for inner growth. As a result, I have had to rebuild myself in a slightly different way, and I have more empathy for others and different insight in my therapy sessions. Many times, I have needed to seek the support of those who have helped ground me, bringing valuable clarity when rejection has taken the wind out of my sails. I'm on a journey with this, and always will be. Rejection still finds me floored at times, but the impact isn't as devastating as it used to be.

When you are rejected, you have a choice. Are you going to let what has happened define you? Are you going to accept this rejection as a statement about your worthiness to be loved, to experience good things, to be vulnerable? Or are you going to stick your armour on and live a half-life hidden in a safe corner? Therapy has been a pertinent part of this process for me, and if any of the rejections you've faced in life has found you hiding in the corner, I would encourage you to seek supportive guidance so that you can build strength to face the risky yet full life that is available for you. (See Helpful Contacts, page 265.)

Coping with rejection

Here are some tips for dealing with that stomach-dropping sense of rejection:

- Allow yourself to feel your emotions, whatever they may be. It's very normal to feel disappointment, frustration, anger, grief or hurt.
- Remind yourself that rejection hurts because it challenges your ego and your self-esteem somehow. You are not weak or irrational because you have feelings.
- Imagine those feelings are a wave. You are in the boat, being tossed around by the emotions. But you are *not in* the water. You are *not* the emotions themselves. Let them move through you and change form and intensity. Don't shame yourself with: 'I shouldn't think/feel this . . .'
- Accept responsibility where it is due, but address misplaced guilt, which leads to increased self-criticism and shame. Use the ACT technique described on pages 117–121.
- Choose to be kind and gentle with yourself, not stubborn or critical. You are only human, and everyone else involved is only human too. We all get it wrong: we all see it, say it and hear it wrong sometimes.
- Ground yourself in the facts. Notice where you have let the rejection form statements about who you are. Introduce an element of uncertainty; for example, the statement 'I am a failure' becomes 'well, that didn't go to plan'.
- Don't dwell on what you 'could' or 'should' have done differently, but ask yourself, 'What might I do differently next time?'
- Remind yourself that feelings aren't facts. You might

feel rubbish, but you are not rubbish. You might feel unloved, but you are not unlovable.

- Speak to someone supportive who can help ground you and bring clarity when the rejection challenges your ability to see things clearly and rationally.
- You will move into a place of acceptance. It will come, but it takes varying amounts of time, depending on the situation.

When I was at university, there was a girl in my class who was always quite dismissive towards me. I'd watch her be warm and friendly to those around me, but I'd sense a coldness from her. I spent hours wondering what I had done wrong, and I put a lot of energy into winning her round. Perhaps if I was nicer, asked her more questions about herself, or bought her a coffee on the way to the lecture, she might change her mind about me? Lo and behold, a few months later, on a night out, she drunkenly proclaimed, 'I've just realised why I didn't really like you! You remind me of my cousin, who used to bully me every summer when we camped together.' Her rejection of me was, in fact, nothing to do with me at all. This served as a stark reminder that sometimes we face rejection due to factors that are completely out of our control. Sometimes they are in our control; sometimes we can amend them; sometimes we can apologise or explain ourselves; sometimes we simply cannot.

No rejection ever compromises your worth.

While rejection may temporarily stamp on your self-esteem, you have the ability to control how much power you give it. No rejection ever compromises your worth. It just shakes your understanding of it. And, thank goodness, you can change that! Oh rejection! I will forever be fighting a battle to keep the fear of it from winning me over. But fear has pushed me into a dark corner for long enough. I want to live where the colour is. Even if the risk resides there too.

To sum up

When we get down to the bare bones of the matter, confidence is simply the ability to be authentic and true to who you are. Now, I know this doesn't feel that simple, but I personally find it very helpful to focus my attention and energy on those small opportunities that lie right in front of me and which allow me to practise being more authentic about my own needs, feelings and opinions. If you set your focus on coaching yourself through these small steps, you'll find that confidence will come in time as a positive side-effect! So, don't seek confidence; seek authenticity instead. As you begin to feel more comfortable being yourself, and start to receive positive feedback for this and your relationships become more enriched, so your self-esteem will increase.

Don't seek confidence; seek authenticity.

You'll become increasingly aware of when these small opportunities to practise authenticity arise. In those moments, I like to quietly challenge myself by asking: 'Should I stay or should I grow?' (Are you singing a popular 1980s punk song now too?) Each opportunity is a chance to stay the same or step out in authenticity and speak out, express a need, assert a boundary or act on something, even when I might be tempted to stay in my comfort zone.

Be kind to yourself as you step out. It takes energy to change and to coach ourselves through situations such as, for example, taking a step to assert a boundary and then being met with a negative response. Our comfort zone is where we feel safe and secure. Sure, not much growth occurs there, but there is a time to stay and a time to grow. You don't need to put pressure on yourself to always choose those risky-feeling leaps.

Remember, growth isn't linear. Consider what else is going on in your life. At times of challenge and change, your resources and energy will be lower, because they're being used to help you make it through. Imagine being on an ocean. When a storm rises and the sea becomes turbulent, it's natural to reach for the safety and relative comfort of a lifeboat, rather than suddenly decide it'd be a great time to learn how to swim! Your self-esteem will be nurtured by small steps of authenticity; the two are intertwined, so trust your instincts and be true to yourself in your actions. Your heartfelt efforts – large or small – will never, ever be in vain.

JOURNAL POINTS

- What does confidence mean to you?
- Who do you view as confident? What does it feel like when you are with that person?
- Has your confidence been fixed on achieving goals? What are those goals?
- Where do you think you are on the introvert–extrovert scale? With this in mind, how might you tweak your boundaries, and what you expect from yourself?
- What small yet authentic-feeling risks might you take?

Chapter 11

The end and the beginning

Mantra: *I can anchor myself in my truths.*

How shall I end this book? I wish I could say something that would make the scales fall from your eyes once and for all, enabling you to see yourself clearly. But I can't. I can only share my tools and thoughts in the hope that, with time, you'll start feeling more and more like an individual who knows she has equal worth to those she values in life. While we might have reached the end of this book, I hope it feels like the beginning of a new chapter for you.

I'm going to leave you with some final words of encouragement to cheer you on your way – and a reminder that this journey really is not a sprint, but a slow-footed, dancing marathon. I want to share my favourite anchoring tool here and then, in chapter 12, you'll discover three pep talks to which you can refer whenever the need arises, so bend those page corners for emergency guidance in those challenging moments.

Find your anchor

Anchor yourself in the truths you know. This next practice is my most favourite tool of all; and I have an anchor tattooed on the inside of my wrist as a prompt to remember it. Because life will constantly try to add on more layers that will have you questioning yourself. And the world and all its people will carry on trying to tell you who you are and what you should believe about your worth and worthiness of good things. So anchor yourself in the truths you know. Let these be the things that tether you to yourself when the storms rage, uncertainty whips up and rejections come your way. Write your truths down in your journal, on your mirror, on your hand.

I will share mine here, but I encourage you to write down your own too.

- I am loved by those who matter most to me.
- I am doing good things.
- My presence is more important than perfection.

These are my truths. You will have yours. Everything else is just noise. Everything else is subjective. Everything else, we can take and question – and either let it go or let it change us, depending on the power we choose to give it. So it's time to seek out and set down those truths of yours – the fundamentals, the things you know for sure about yourself – and when the world or your self-esteem feels like it's wavering, stand firmly upon them.

Question your own beliefs

It didn't even occur to me that perhaps I was wrong about myself, but questioning it was like turning on a light.

Fiona

I have mentioned earlier in this book how I don't like to be wrong, and that I like to think I know myself best of all. I prefer to believe that what I think about myself is true, because to have that perception questioned challenges the truth of my thoughts and the way that I see the world. It's not comfortable to be reminded that perhaps the way we see ourselves, or view situations, isn't exactly right. It shakes the foundations of our awareness and questions our ability to make sense of the world. But if you acknowledge that the way other people see you is based on their own assumptions, which are shaped by factors outside of your control, then you must also acknowledge that the way you see yourself is based on your own past experiences and assumptions too. You see everything through that lens – others, yourself and the world itself!

It can feel uncomfortable to contemplate that the way you see yourself might not tally with the truth. However, with that discomfort comes the sheer hope that perhaps you are actually a much nicer and more worthy person that you have been led to believe. Perhaps if your assumption that you are inherently a failure, undeserving of good things, is wrong ... then maybe there's a possibility that you are inherently a good person who deserves good things. Maybe you've been viewing yourself unfavourably through the scratched, smeared lens of low self-esteem all along.

So, notice your beliefs and opinions about yourself and what others think of you, and consider the fact that these beliefs and opinions may not be factual. Introduce some uncertainty into the statements you make about yourself: in this way, 'they will laugh at me' can turn into 'they may or may not laugh at me'; 'I'll get it wrong' becomes 'I may or may not get it wrong'; 'I can't do this' changes to 'maybe I could do this', and 'nobody likes me' is replaced by 'some people may not like me, some people may'.

If, for example, your biggest fear is coming across as awkward, inject some clarity into that belief. Let's pick it apart for a moment.

1. I might act in a way I personally consider to be awkward. Yet the person I'm talking to doesn't get that impression.
2. I may act in a way I don't deem to be awkward, and another person might experience me as awkward.
3. I act as I act, and the other person may not be thinking anything about me at all!

We cannot pre-empt how we will be perceived.

You can apply this approach to many different fears. It introduces an element of uncertainty where perhaps before you were approaching a situation as if your fears were unquestionable truths, not possibilities. We cannot pre-empt how we will be perceived. People view each of us through their own lenses, and they are so subjective!

Can you imagine how hard you'd have to work to appeal

to a large crowd of people? It would be virtually impossible. You'd tell a joke and 70 per cent of the audience might laugh hysterically; 20 per cent of them might groan and roll their eyes; and 10 per cent of the crowd might not get it at all. Now, does that say more about your ability to tell a good joke, or about the myriad different lenses that people view the world through? What might make me laugh might not make you laugh. What I experience as awkward might be different to what you feel is awkward. What hurts me might not hurt you. What confuses me might not confuse you. What excites me might not excite you. My reactions reflect who I am as an individual, and are not a reflection of you.

So the next time you find yourself automatically believing what your thoughts are telling you, call this to question and seek out the facts. Because often the cold, hard facts of the matter are a little kinder and more self-esteem boosting for us than our old, unchallenged narratives!

Set achievable goals

If I want to change something about myself, I want to do it yesterday.

Anne

When it comes to your aims and hopes for growth and change, it can be really motivating and good for your self-esteem to see some progress. However, ensure that you are kind in your goal-setting. Consider the pressure you are putting on yourself and the likelihood of being able to meet your goals. If you have perfectionist qualities, be aware of how this might play out in relation to your aims and goals.

I remember when I began to address my internal dialogue. As soon as I realised that I was effectively carrying around an inner bully and listening intently to everything it yelled in my ear, I wanted it gone. I worked hard at challenging my thoughts, and I felt an intense sense of frustration and failure when I realised some of them had nevertheless slipped through the net. When you are trying to change a pattern of behaviour, especially one that has been a habit for a long while, it's important to treat yourself with patience and compassion.

It's important to afford yourself patience and compassion.

Inner growth isn't a linear process, it's bumpy and sometimes uncomfortable. Stop expecting shiny, smooth lines of trajectory towards your goal. You are only human and there are many other factors at play. Heaping on high expectations only piles on more pressure. And pressure can sit very heavily on our shoulders. Confidence is a muscle that will grow when you step incrementally outside of your comfort zone. Imagine if I signed up for a marathon tomorrow without training first – I'd be setting myself up for a cruel fail. Training takes time, run by run, during which our muscle fibres will tear and rebuild. Yet don't we place this kind of demand and expectation on ourselves all the time in other ways?

Continuing to journal can be very helpful, as it means we can look back and see how far we've come, one baby step at a time. The other day, I hopped in the car and drove thirty minutes down the motorway. Uneventful? Exactly. That was precisely what was so astounding about my journey. In the past, I'd experienced such intense anxiety when driving that I didn't actually get behind the wheel for almost a decade! The fact that I'd got into the car and driven to a friend's house in a boring, uneventful manner helped to remind me of my growth. A few short years ago, the mere prospect of driving would have caused me so much stress, fear and sleeplessness that I'd have probably made an excuse and cancelled the visit.

When you notice something that makes you realise how far you have come, encourage yourself to feel proud of those moments. Those moments are victories. Celebrate them! They may seem insignificant to others, but that's because we are all growing in many different areas of life at many different rates.

Final words

We've reached the end of this book, but in so many ways I hope it marks a beginning for you. I hope that you've begun to realise just how valid your needs and feelings are, and how worthy of good things you are. As you continue to challenge those layers of fear and worry about what other people think, they will loosen their grip and their power over you. It will happen over time, not overnight.

You didn't ever really need fixing, just revealing.

Refer back to the words in these pages whenever you need to, and let them sink in and become part of your support in wobbly moments. Keep on keeping on – because, as I said at the very start of this book, the best, most life-giving growth actually involves a chipping away, a stripping back to the core of what was there all along. Quite frankly, you didn't ever really need fixing, just revealing.

You're doing this.

Chapter 12

Three emergency pep talks

I want to leave you with three pep talks that you can turn to whenever you need to. There are times in my life when I just need someone to put their hands on my shoulders and help me find my way back to grounded rationality; and these peptalks are for when you have those exact same moments. Perhaps you feel overwhelmed, or guilt, rejection or burnout are clouding your understanding of your worth. I want you to imagine that someone who cares about you has placed their hands reassuringly on your shoulders, and is speaking these words to you with confidence and gentleness.

Feeling guilty

Let's take a look at that guilt. What sparked it for you? Was it a sudden feeling or have you been feeling like this for a while? Either way, let's address it now. First of all, I want to remind you that just because you feel guilty, it doesn't mean that you are. The guilt isn't there to make you feel like a bad person, so let's ensure it doesn't stay sat in your stomach to fuel self-criticism and push your self-esteem down. I want you to imagine that guilt as a sooty rock in your hand. Tell me, what is it for? What would a judge say in court if you came to him with the lump of coal and asked for his verdict? Would he judge you guilty?

Now, regardless of how deserving you feel or not, we need to introduce some compassion into the situation. What would you tell a friend if they came to you with that sooty rock? How would you make them feel better? This isn't about removing responsibility where it may be due; it's just about bringing some balance into the situation. It's about respecting the fact that you are only human and you get it wrong. There are limits to your resources, like there are for everyone.

What is this guilt prompting you to do? Perhaps it's prompting you to address your self-esteem, or to change a boundary if you're feeling guilty because you think you 'should' be doing more, or you 'shouldn't' have said no to someone? Perhaps it's prompting you to ask someone for forgiveness, or maybe even to forgive yourself? Maybe it's about a practical action, finishing a job or rejigging priorities?

Now that you know what you need to do, act on this prompting if you can – and then let that guilt go. It has served its purpose. Keep letting it go when it rises up. It isn't there to shame you. You do not need to punish yourself, so be wary of where self-criticism and self-sabotage creep in. You are not the exception to the rule that everyone is worthy of compassion.

Feeling rejected

I know rejection feels uncomfortable, and it's likely that feelings of shame have been triggered for you. We need to separate out the fact that just because you've faced rejection, this doesn't mean that you aren't enough. Whatever the circumstances you've faced, the rejection relates to only a very small part of the entirety of who you are.

What are your truths? Remember the things that anchor you? You know you are loved by those who matter to you. Therefore, you are lovable. That is a fact. Just because a part of you hasn't been accepted, it does not mean that you, as a person, are unacceptable. Keep reminding yourself of that truth. Rejection can feel like a fog that descends, clouding out rationality. Fog dissipates and lifts, so hold on to what you know whilst your vision is blurred, grab on to those anchoring truths of yours and repeat them to yourself like mantras to remind you that you are safe. You might feel ashamed but you are not shameful.

Let those feelings of hurt or disappointment come and go. Don't try to fix or change them; they are what they are. Rejection hurts, but hurt passes and you only have to look over your life to remind yourself that the intensity of feelings comes and goes.

You may have been rejected, but try now not to reject yourself. Acknowledge your needs and continue to meet them. You do not need to punish yourself. If the fog isn't lifting, turn to someone who can help bring clarity to the situation for you, and support you through this. Don't stay in the fog; you are worthy of a hand to guide you out of it.

Feeling burnt out

You must feel exhausted. We need to look at that gap between your load and your limit. Have you been carrying too much? Have you been buying into the message that your worth is the sum of what you do and how well you do it? You are only one person, with limited energy and emotional and physical resources. The levels of these change every day and you absolutely need to be topping them up. Have you been resting? I know life is busy, full and fast, but you are not a machine. In fact, even machines need servicing, rebooting and refuelling. Is there anything you can delegate to someone else? If not, is there a corner you can cut, a standard that can be lowered, or some space that can be made so that you can recharge?

Perhaps what is exhausting you isn't the load, but the mental pressure you put upon yourself to get things right all the time? Perhaps it's the threat of criticism or self-rejection if you don't. If you wouldn't speak to or treat a loved one in the way you are speaking to or treating yourself, this approach is not good enough for you either. Maybe you need to monitor whether you're respecting yourself in these areas.

The antidote to this burnt-out feeling is to take a moment to ask yourself what your needs are. What three things do you need? Name them. How might you go some way towards meeting those needs? Your needs matter very much. Very much. They matter as much as the needs of others that you've been prioritising. Every time you give out, this costs you something – and you deserve much more than to live life out of the bottom of a scraped-out barrel.

Helpful contacts

If you want to take the things you have been exploring in this book further, here are some potential next steps and contacts:

The People-pleasing course

This is a three-week, self-led course addressing people-pleasing, perfectionism, confidence and emotional resilience.

I was a people-pleaser for most of my life until I got sick of being in a cycle of burning out. I repeatedly gave too much of myself away, leaving only the dregs to keep me going. I knew I didn't want to spend the rest of my life living in a way that was so damaging to my sense of worth and identity. I started a process of addressing this, and as a result, I feel more 'me' than I ever have. I have interwoven my psychological insight and experience as a therapist, along with my personal learning, so that I can gently challenge you on a habit of a lifetime. See my website (annamathur.com) for a full description and reviews.

The Reframing Anxiety course

This is a three-week, self-led course suitable for anyone experiencing any level of anxiety.

Anxiety can rob you of enjoyment of the good things in your life. It whispers, 'what if?' and sets your mind wandering down a path of scenarios that may never happen. This course is full of both professional and personal insight, to help you change the way you deal with your anxiety, and guide you towards reclaiming your power and headspace. See my website (annamathur.com) for a full description and reviews.

NHS and low-cost therapy

Your doctor may be able to refer you for six–twelve sessions of NHS-funded therapy. This might be face to face or using an online format. The waiting times and the services are dependent on area.

For low-cost therapy, search for services local to you. There might be charities, churches or training institutes that offer no-cost or low-cost sessions that you can access.

Private therapy

The Counselling Directory 'find a therapist' function is my go-to recommendation for finding a therapist. It allows you to search using your postcode and browse the profiles of therapists in your area.

NHS website

The NHS website is a brilliant resource for learning about all things mental and physical relating to health. It offers advice on where to seek support and other next steps you might like to take in addressing any symptoms.

Supportive websites based in the UK

Mentalhealth.org.uk
Mind.org.uk
Samaritans.org.uk
Sane.org.uk

Telephone helplines (UK)

Mind: 0300 123 3393
Rethink Mental Illness: 0808 8010525
Samaritans: 116 123

Acknowledgements

I wrote this book amidst a global pandemic, and it has brought home to me that so often in life we look at what others have achieved, without knowing the cost or being privy to the support that they have had behind the scenes.

I want to take a moment to thank those who have made writing these words possible. But also, in writing this book I have uncovered quite how life-changing the journey of discovering my worth has been for me. Years ago, I'd have tackled a momentous task like this alone, juggling a busy household, working late, deprioritising rest and exercise. It would have had a high and very hidden cost. But instead, I knew I could lean on those around me, for practical and emotional support. And lean I did.

Thank you to my husband Tarun, for orchestrating things at home so that I could have windows of space to get my head into the words. You know how much this journey of worth has transformed me, and you really 'get' my passion to facilitate and support others through it, too. You made this possible.

Ella, you are part of our family and it is an immense

privilege to have you at the helm of childcare during my work days. I know my children are loved deeply and attended to by you in the hours I've spent upstairs working!

My wonderful mum: thank you for your constant, grounding comfort. You are always at the end of the phone for me, a steady rock to reach for when things feel unsteady. Thank you for cheerleading me along the way, always.

Lauren, my agent: I said this last time with *Mind Over Mother*, and I'll say it again. Thank you for being my guide along this book journey. It's been such a new experience to navigate, but it's reassuring to know that with your amazing skill and insight, I have you lighting the way!

Zoe, my editor: I know that *Know Your Worth* has a great home in your team. I highly appreciate the guidance and knowledge you and your team bring to my work. Thank you for taking a chance on me again. I want to make you proud!

Deborah, my therapist: your steadfast insight, encouragement and support as I commit to working on my self-esteem is invaluable.

Finally, to Oscar, Charlie and Florence – my three cheeky peaches: you concrete my reason for continuing to do this work and share this work. I want you to be sure of your value and I know that the best way to model that is by ensuring I continue to seek my own through the chaos and noise of life. I want to live more authentically so that you are not afraid to be yourselves.

Index